"NO MAN LOVES LIFE THAN HIM THAT IS GROWING OLD"
- Sophocles

"APPLIES TO WOMEN TOO!"
- Helene

For Zaf, With Love

Who retired once and went back to work. Who retired again and went back to work. Who retired for the third time, when I semi-retired and we embarked on our retirement journey together.

Here is the story in words and pictures on how we began to explore retirement and continue to do so at home and on our travels.
Each day is a good day – we have health, we have faith, we have family, we have friends and we have each other.

ISBN: 979-8-9911564-0-0 (Paper) | 979-8-9911564-1-7 (E-Book)

Library of Congress Control Number: TXu 2-435-000

For privacy reasons, some names, locations, and dates may have been changed.

Photos by Helene K. Liatsos

First edition distribution 2024.

www.retirementexplored.com

TABLE OF CONTENTS

Introduction

When I started Retirement Explored, it all began as we were going through the pain of downsizing. We made the decision to simplify our lives by living smaller - yet larger in a different way.

We began to rid ourselves of "stuff" that had accumulated over the decades and was basically just taking up space. This was not easy. What to do with the various items we'd collected over the years was the big question. As we moved through the steps of discarding, donating, and/or keeping, I thought: "Well, we can't be the only ones going through this!"

Going online and searching under the word Retirement, I was astounded to see the hundreds of sites, posts, and various information in general. Aha! There are people out there who are just like us. And so, the idea of a personal blog about our own retirement journey was created.

Our mission: To Share Our Own Retirement Experience to Inspire, Motivate, and Enthuse other Retirees and Soon to Be Retired. I believe that just because we are retired, doesn't mean we have to act like that! Society likes to fit people like us into a book. I am here to explore and break that mold.

Retire-Agers™

If you relate to this or simply want to learn more about our journey, I encourage you to keep reading. In keeping with my original thought about others who are facing retirement or have retired, the concept of interviewing them was conceived. As I was putting my thoughts together about what this would entail, I started to think about the words that describe us: seniors, elderly, aged, old, over the hill, etc. These struck me as us being feeble and doddering. Visions of us sitting by a window, with a blanket on our knees filled my head and this was all wrong! We are vital, we are energetic, and we are bubbly and busy! I played around with some ideas and decided on Retire-Agers™. If teenagers can have their own terms, then so can we!

The first person I selected was my brother-in-law, Jerry. He was in the early stages of dementia, so it was urgent for me to tell his story. I gently prodded him to tell me about his retirement and he told me what he could. I added what I knew from his life with my sister for close to 50 years. His story is now a memorial as he succumbed to his illness in July 2020.

As we sat together, I noticed his hands in repose. They were the legacy of his work. All work begins in the mind, but it is executed through the hands. This is how our work lives. As I type this, I am using my brain to formulate the thoughts and the words, but I am using my hands to type them. To me, this is more important than the face. I see the strength and depth of the work he had done. He is a perfect example of the Retire-Agers™ I have interviewed to date.

There have also been many other friends and colleagues who have joined me in sharing their journeys. I will recount some of these stories in this book so you can gain perspective on the vitality that lives in each of us - no matter our age.

What You Can Expect From This Book:

When I began writing my blogs, they were crafted so readers could identify with their own thoughts and actions about retirement. While they read closely to my own personal story - how it happened for us, how we made the decisions we did, how we overcame obstacles in the process, and how we are living the retirement life now - each chapter stands alone as its own chapter in this story. Yet each one is connected to the others where they all play into the narrative of what it means to explore retirement. This book will shed light on behind the scenes of writing my blogs with additional comments, thoughts, and of course, the photos to add visual impact and tell the story behind our retirement journey.

ABOUT

Meet The RETIRE-AGERS™ – Helene and Zaf!

Zaf and I measure time from the day we met, when the road turned for both of us.

I was born in Lamia, smack in the middle of Central Greece and was carried into NYC when I was 9 months old. I did not know a word of English when I went to kindergarten, but the streets of Manhattan were my playground, teaching me how to speak like a New Yawker! Soon after, my parents placed me in private Greek school, where I became fluent in the Greek language and obtained a strong background in Greek history, geography, and mythology. Our first trip back to Greece was when I was young girl; it gave me the opportunity to see the ancient ruins. I burst into tears at the realization that I belonged to this beautiful land. My first career was then in the travel industry, allowing me to travel extensively and establishing a life-long love of it. After moving to Los Angeles, it placed me in the perfect place to meet Zaf.

Zaf was born in Nea Mehaniona, a small village outside of Thessaloniki, in Northern Greece and came to the USA when he was ten years old. He assimilated quickly by playing soccer with the local kids on the streets of East Orange, NJ. His athletic ability was recognized by a full college scholarship. Marrying young and raising three children, he worked several jobs a week to make end meets and finish his education. It paid off when he reached executive level in a major convenience store company overseeing over 130 franchises. Life changed 30 years later when he moved to Phoenix, AZ as a consultant, setting up a household of one. And then again, when he moved to Southern California several years later.

Zaf and I met in 2005 on a Greek online dating site – I know, I know – we took a chance. We both wanted to connect with someone who knew and understood our ethnic background. Going back to where we came from, we found what we were looking for. We took one look at each other, recognized each other, and married each other. The Greek Gods were smiling upon us.

Almost immediately, we discovered we are both drawn to foreign countries. Perhaps it was because we were raised in an immigrant family where the language, the food, customs, and traditions were so different than our American friends next door. In any event, we began to travel, continue to travel and is the focal point of our retirement plans and hence, this book.

You will find, through the stories of our trip, that while we both agree on when to retire and some aspects of retirement itself, like moving out of the current house and some travel plans, you will also find that we each have our own personal vision of how retirement will unfold.

Come along with us as we reveal the negotiations and compromises of what our retirement will look like!

We are on it!

www.retirementexplored.com

WELCOME TO OUR RETIREMENT STORY!

Originally Published:

October 28, 2019

My husband Zaf and I are Retire-Agers™ wannabee's!
"Retirement" thinking has been part of our lives for the past several years, but we haven't taken that leap yet. We are exploring our options to see what would be right for us, and then we will be exploring retirement as we live it!

Timing is a big part of retirement planning. For us, it will be on March 1, 2021 - that will be the date when we will leave the hard work, the headaches, and the "hurrying" of life to adopt an easier way of living.

There is much to consider and much to do. A household of "stuff" to be dealt with. The house itself. A business we own and a career to minimize. We also need to decide where we will live next and what to do with all this free time we will have. Travel looms large as it has been part of our lives already and something we truly enjoy.

New information on "how to" retire comes to us almost everyday. Financial planning, 55+ housing developments, ways to de-clutter our homes, saving tips, senior discounts, senior travel, senior medical advances to make us feel and perform younger, etc. There is so much out there and so much to explore!

We will be sharing our challenges and our discoveries as we move towards the big day! After that, we will cover how we spend our days with activities, travel, and whatever else comes along!

Our hope is that you will find our journey funny, inspiring, and of value as you prepare for your retirement.

We invite you to part of our journey.

WE ARE ON IT!

Originally Published:

October 28, 2019

▬▬▬▬

We are ready to retire! The countdown is upon us. It seems like it happened overnight, but it has taken four+ decades to arrive at the door of a brand new way of life.

Living takes time. Each day we have lived has brought us closer to the day where we make the changes to go on at a different pace and at a different place, doing different things and exploring the world near us and far, far away.

2021! Save the date!

We will retire; that's what we plan, we expect, we hope and pray for. I spend lots of time exploring retirement options: where will we live, where would we travel to, what to do every day, how to make new friends should we move to another city, etc. My husband is Zaf leaves all the exploring to me. That's not to say he doesn't have an opinion. He does weigh in after I present the question and a couple of answers; then the negotiating begins!

Retirement is not a one-size fits all. We each have a vision of what we expect will happen. In most ways, we are synchronized. In others, we need to compromise and find the right fit. Our individual personalities, our like and dislikes, our preferences and choices make up a complex meshing of two people into one cohesive unit. My dad once said that marriage was two horses pulling one cart; indeed, it has proven to be true.

The fun part is the exploration of how it will all come together. We invite you to join in! We promise you some insight, laughter, and the joy of knowing that sharing life's adventures is what we can each do for each other that makes life interesting.

I'M NOT IN A HURRY

Originally Published:

October 28, 2019

Roadrunner – that would be a good definition for me. Blessed with a very high energy level, I did three or more things at once… while thinking about the next three or more things that had to be done. My dad used to call me the "hurricane" because I would come into a room in a whirlwind, stirring everyone and everything up.

For years, I ran everywhere. Seeing two or more clients a day, grocery shopping, cooking and cleaning up after dinner, paying bills, doing the laundry, etc. – my metabolism was on overdrive. Even when my body was at rest, my mind was racing from one thought to another. I had always been a night owl; sleep was elusive. Dragging myself out of bed in the morning was a chore but once I was up, I hit the floor running.

Well, now things are different. For one thing, I wake up at 5:30 or 6:00am. It doesn't matter if I fall asleep quickly or not; it doesn't matter if I wake up a couple of times during the night. My inner clock has changed me into being an early riser. By 1:00 pm, I'm beat.

I began to sense that I am slowing down physically and mentally a while ago. The aches and pains arrived. A disc out of whack creates great lower back pain; arthritis is here. As my body is aging, I find that I get tired more often and need to rest. It takes me longer to do things I was able to do in a snap; it takes me longer to answer those quiz questions on game shows you see every night. I can "see" the answer in my head, but often can't remember the name of it.

At first, I was in denial and just ran harder… as I explored this phenomenon, I realized that "hey – its all good!" It took me a while to accept this as I often felt that I was not "on top of things going on in the world." And then one day, it finally dawned on me. I'm okay with this because I will never be on top of things; the world is on a different timetable than me.

I am not in a hurry any more. There is no reason for it. I've got a "new normal." Work has evolved to a different level so I can pace myself with client needs. I work at home so there is no mad dash out the door in the morning. I am not standing at the deli counter tapping my toe exasperated with the slow worker behind the counter; I now chit chat with the other customers or peruse the displays of salamis and hams while waiting for my order. If I catch myself dashing from one thing to another, I purposefully stop what I'm doing, take a deep breath, and begin again with smaller, slower steps.

Each day has a different rhythm to it. I plan my day's activities: work, chores, errands, etc. based on what absolutely must get done vs. can I do this tomorrow? I take naps when I want to. As Zaf too is slowing down and has his share of aging issues (total knee replacement!), we have simplified how we live our lives to smaller, simpler meals, hiring out more household maintenance and chores, etc. The Greek word Ataraxia means: a state of freedom from emotional disturbance and anxiety; tranquility. I have this word posted on my desk blotter because that's our goal.

I am reserving my energy and taking care of myself (and Zaf!) because when we retire, we're going to explore the world. There are so many places we want to see, and we need to be in decent shape so we can walk through the picturesque villages in Italy and Portugal, visit ancient ruins and modern museums, taste different foods and dance to the tunes of the local lutes, bagpipes and clarinets.

Living takes time. And it's time for me to now do what I want to do and that is exploring retirement. When we get to the point (not too far away now!) that we can actually "retire," I will be sharing our explorations online. The thought of that makes me very happy.

NO, THANK YOU. I'M RETIRED

Originally Published:

October 28, 2019

There have three distinct times when I have used the word "No" incessantly when I didn't want to do something.

As a toddler, it was useful when I did not want to eat spinach, take a nap, or go potty. It was the favorite word to use to aggravate my parents and attempt to control the outcome of what they wanted me to do versus what I wanted to do.

In my early 30's, I rediscovered the word No… as in: "I'm 32 years old! I don't have to do this!" Being a "yes person," I had found myself doing things I really didn't want to do, going places I didn't want to go because I didn't want to be "left out". Or I worried about what people would say if I stopped going, as in "what…is she avoiding us?" or "does she think she's above us?" This was causing me a great deal of anxiety.

I had stumbled across the book, "The Road Less Traveled" (maybe stumbling is not the right word; maybe its just the universe giving me what I needed when I needed it – providence!) I picked it up and read it right through to the end in one setting, highlighting every other sentence. It taught me that it is okay to say no, firmly and warmly. It taught me that saying no is powerful in keeping me mentally and emotionally sane. Perfect! So, I began to use the concept. It wasn't so easy at first, but eventually, it served me well in response to bullying bosses and/or co-workers, toxic friendships, romances, and when my mother said: "When are you going to get married?"

Now, as I am inching towards retirement and exploring how to simplify our lives, it has been re-purposed into: NO! I'm retired! I don't have to wear high heels or business clothes. I don't need the latest gadgets and electronics. I don't care about the inane TV shows or award ceremonies. I don't have to be present in other people's activities every day – I can chose when to get involved and when to stay home.

My social media is meeting a friend for coffee, lunch, walk, or a day at the beach, park, library. The entire universe does not need to know what I do with my time: what my dinner looks like or the sunset from my window.

Happy to report that, although, I am "friends" with many people, I don't "follow" but a few. I hesitate to "like" something because I don't want to get their postings every minute of the day. Selfish? Perhaps a tad – I look at it as maintaining peace and quiet in my brain and soul. The value of saying no is first step. Being okay with saying no is the second one.

I use personal social media for close family and friends only. And I will use it for my blog, of course – because the people who connect with me there are just like me – preparing to retire, retired, traveling, cooking, gardening, bowling, dancing, etc. We are the Retire-Agers™!

A long time ago, when I was in my 20's, I saw a famous actress on a nightly talk show. She was in her late 80's and was a spitfire. I clearly remember her saying that she says what she wants to say and does what she wants to do because "who is gonna argue with an old lady?" I have also experienced, first-hand, men and women in their advanced years who do the very same thing. They are outspoken, spunky, and fearless. When I grow up, I want to be just like them!

I don't want to be bogged down with "should's – there is nothing I should be doing when I retire other than being retired. I did my thing, put in my time, paid my dues so now, I want to take advantage of the freedom that comes with retirement. Each day will open to a world of exploration: what is going on down at the library? Should we go to the farmer's market and get fresh blueberries? The senior center is having Taco Tuesday! Let's cut down some lemons from our tree and make lemonade!

I don't need anything more because the real blessing in using the word NO, is that I have learned that I have enough.

ONE SIZE DOES NOT FIT BOTH OF US

Originally Published:

October 28, 2019

We are at the point of "exploring" retirement. We talk about it, think about it, and daydream about it. It is exciting to know that we can do whatever we want (mostly!). We read/hear/see others talk about their "second act," "a new chapter," "the best is yet to come," etc. We prefer to call it Freedom.

This exploration certainly includes financials, but all that being in place, the "What do we do all day?" looms larger. Zaf had retired once, about ten years ago. His new schedule was golf two times a week. One day a week, he would jump on his Harley and head for the Santa Monica Mountains. It was relaxing for him, but I had the cell phone glued to my ear all day long wondering if/when it would ring with an accident report. The other days would be spent on his computer until 11:00AM in his robe! The list of chores was on his desk, but it was slow going. This routine lasted about three months - golf was not as interesting anymore and the bike was safe and warm in the garage. It was time to re-think this retirement thing.

All the subtle hints I gave him about how retirement without a plan is depressing, how it's fattening if you sit around all day, how it ages you quickly, etc. made no impact. I repeated often that you have to have a purpose when you wake up each morning – something to do and/or someplace to go. I pointed out several friends who retired and were miserable. He agreed but seemed paralyzed as to what to do.

Using the Internet, I found a part-time job that was right up his alley. From 9 to 1, 5 days a week, about 25 minutes from the house. I printed it out and placed it on his desk saying, "I think these people need you." He sighed, called, and he got the job - a new man emerged. That was a perfect gig for him; it opened new doors and he is currently working in his field at a full-time job that he absolutely loves.

I continue to work. I truly love what I do working at home and have a very flexible schedule. It hasn't always been that way of course; I had to build my business and get it to the point where it is today. 95% of the work I do is online allowing me to work in my shorts and a T-shirt, drink hot/cold beverages all day long, and take an afternoon nap! Zaf had to be trained not to call me between 1 and 3!

Retirement for Zaf is: "I'm done! And really mean it this time!" Retirement for me is: "Okay, I'll work at 50% until my brain gives out". I like staying busy and enjoy working with my clients (some of them) so since I can do it from anywhere in the world where there is Internet, why not continue? More money = more travel!

That's the beauty of retirement – we can design it, shape it, and create it to our own liking. The one thing that we do agree on is our love of travel so that will be our focus!

We are on it!

TRAVEL EXPLORED

Originally Published:

October 28, 2019

Explorers were the first travelers. They were the most daring and adventurous who set out to discover new lands, new people, and new experiences. They created the routes that allow us to touch the world. Zaf and I are following in their footsteps.

There was always a sense of wanderlust for me, even as a child. I would dream of far off places that I would visit dressed in sophisticated clothes and dark sun-glasses. What was interesting to me was how the people lived. I remember a school geography assignment where we had to pick a country and describe it. Everyone but me wrote about the latitude, longitude, the weather, and the gross national product. I wrote about the food they ate, the style of clothes they wore, how they made their living, what the schools were like, etc. I got an A! The everyday living was crucial to understanding them. I knew that back then and this keen interest about people is what excites me about travel now.

Zaf and I did some traveling on our own before we were married and together we have done even more. Right after our first trip, I bought a journal with a picture of an airplane, a ship, a motorcycle, and various cameras. The wording on it says: Jetset, Travel, Bon Voyage, World Traveler and Let's Go! It has a kind of old-world, yet funky look to it. In it, I have recorded every trip Zaf and I have taken together, even little weekend getaways. I record the dates, itinerary, names of hotel/ships, restaurants, historical sites, activities, interesting people we meet along the way, etc.

Retirement is the perfect time to reach my goal of filling up this journal, beginning a new one and several more after that. We will be free from daily responsibilities, from a scheduled lifestyle, from deadlines and the pressure to meet them. We will be free to roam around the world.

We welcome you to our travels: past, present and future. The more we explore, the more we will share. Don't ask me how we are doing. Ask me, "Where are you now?"

OUR RETIREMENT KICKOFF

Originally Published:

October 28, 2019

2021 – Save the Retirement Date!

Yes, we retired but…

We don't want to have a do-nothing retirement. It doesn't sound like much fun. We just want to get rid of the daily responsibility of work, maintaining a big house, fighting traffic and the like. When all of this goes away, we will be free! All the stress of juggling, scheduling, problem solving, and technology challenges (!) will be replaced with simpler days and lots of adventure.

A whole new world is out there… not just in travel but in the everyday things we do. We will simply replace the old things we used to do with new things we can discover and do. It will be a continuation of our lives in another direction. The last time I went to the movies in the middle of the day was when I was sixteen. We inquired about joining a bowling league at our church, but they start on 9:00pm on a Wednesday night – not good for us when we get up at 6:00am and go off to work! These two activities will be like dating all over again; I can't wait to tell Zaf!

Our goal is to spend the first six months or so living and traveling in Greece as well as other parts of Europe and the Middle East. When we get back home, we will settle into our new home which we have no idea where it will be as of right now!

One of my big projects I am planning is to sort all the photographs I've collected over my lifetime, as well as my mother's and aunt's. Looking through them, I reminisce - I cry and I laugh. I explain to Zaf what was going on when the picture was taken and who everyone is as he rolls his eyes… because he has heard the stories a few times before! But for me, the pictures and the stories (for both of us!) are the badges of how far we have come… and making the plans to get out into the world is the pathway to how far we still have to go.

As I post our retirement activities – and may there be many – traveling, cooking, dancing, bowling, etc. I want to look back at them one day and say "What happened to retirement?!!!" We will retire from work, but not from life!

And in life, you just never know what can happen, so we must be eager, energized and excited! We will become explorers!

RETIRE-AGERS™

Originally Published:

October 28, 2019

Introducing: Retire-Agers™!

Why don't we have a better word for people who have lived five decades or more? We are called senior citizens, old people, mature adults, old-timers, the elderly, the aging population, old-farts, geezers, etc. And, while all of them may be true (or not!), they are depressing, negative, and in some cases, downright rude!

Words mean things; people create an image in their head about it. These definitions depict someone who is shuffling along, disoriented, and befuddled. With all due respect to those ill and unwell, the babies of the 30's, 40's, 50's and 60's are booming!

We need a word that is a little more perky, positive, and encouraging. We need a word that describes who we are today. Toddlers, teen-agers, 30-somethings, mid-lifers, etc. have their own meaning of where they are in life and so should we - with a better snapshot of a wider and more varied representation of our ever-growing population.

We possess the joy of living; we explore, we travel, we golf, we volunteer, we work, we baby-sit, we care for others, we bowl, we knit, we blog, we exercise, we bake, we play cards, and we dance! We are not going to roll over and play dead until we are dead! Our age is our strength; we have knowledge and experience that is real and authentic. Search engines don't know everything – people need to talk to someone who is original to life. And that is us!

Growing old is inevitable - growing up is not mandatory!

Retire-Agers™! That's the term I came up with to describe who we are; I hope you like it and agree to use it!

You will be meeting Retire-ages throughout this book. Those who worked hard their whole lives, building a career, raising families, helping others, and living a full life with all its ups and downs; these people are now retired. Well deserved.

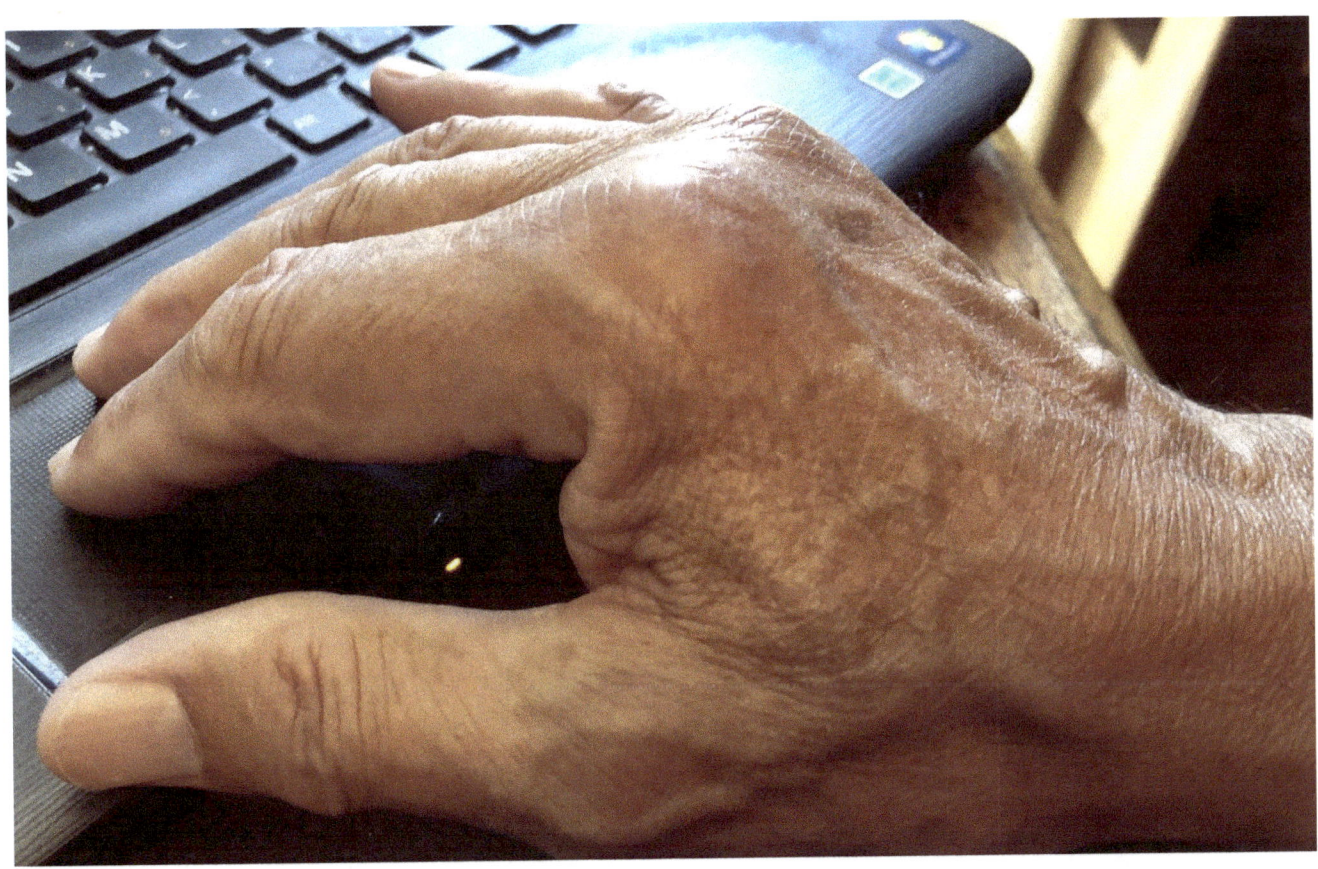

Did they plan their retirement? Or were they forced out of the labor force? Fell ill? Had to caretake a loved one? How do they feel about being retired? What do they do all day? Are they happy they retired or do they regret it? Do they want to go back to work? Can they go back to work? How does a working spouse handle a non-working spouse? Or the other way around? Did they downsize? Did they move to another city? Are they annoying their children and grand-children?

Each story makes its own impact because each story is real. It captures a person's moment in life where they share their thoughts and feelings about being retired. And because each person's story matters, it is important to record it.

Interviewing each of the retirees gave me enormous pleasure and respect of them. Fascinating, funny, poignant, sad, curious, and naughty describes just some of the interesting people I've met so far. So many more of you out there; I can't wait to meet you!

These hands represent how we got the work done. The veins, the age spots, the crinkly skin is who we are. They represent life.

SCROLLING

Originally Published:

October 28, 2019

As I try to stay busy exploring what retirement will be for me and Zaf, a moment of realization on how old I am is when I keep scrolling down (way down!) to pick the year of my birth when filling out an online form… yikes!

Some days I feel it; other days I feel like a much younger person. A lot depends on how I slept the night before or if I have too much work on my desk and am overwhelmed. It might also depend on hearing news of someone the same age as me who is sick or has left us behind.

Still other ways age becomes a reality is when I see the grand-children grow, almost overnight, into young adults. They share their experiences or view of the world in general and I immediately flash to a moment when I too had that experience. My eleven year-old grand-niece, the other day, winced and made a face when she overheard my conversation with her mom, my niece, about me taking a walk that morning at 6:30am – how brisk and fresh the morning felt, how clean the world seemed to be, how alive I felt, etc. I vividly remember having that very same reaction when I heard my parents talking about getting up early to get to work, do the chores, or run the errands. At that age, sleeping in until 9 or 10am was the norm; now, getting up at 5 or 6am is what I do.

There is so much out there that we read or hear on the TV about how aging is just a number, or we are as young you feel, and so on. Anti-aging diets, medicines, exercises, creams and lotions are hawked ad nauseum. They are selling hopes and wishes, in my opinion. What works for me is my mental health. Accepting my age is the first step. Eating smart and getting some physical movement going follows closely. Being clean and dressing appropriately is on the list too.

The key is energy – at this point, I only have energy for the things that make me happy. Work is a big part, but it is finally manageable; simplifying household chores is happening; planning for retirement makes me smile. Giving myself tasks and projects to keep me occupied is a daily effort – some days I do them and some days I don't. I find that I need to pace myself and include resting times. I don't have the same upbeat energy for things I have no interest in.

Being satisfied with my life inspires me and allows me to be curious. Curiosity motivates me to research into ideas we could bring into our life: discover new destinations to travel to, join a yoga class, volunteer at the local shelter, go to the theater more often, etc. It's all out there and awaits us.

Exploring what more we can do is divided into two sections. One is what we can do now (in our spare time) and the other is what we can do when we retire. I try not to think about what condition we might be in when that happens, but I hope and pray for the best. Either way, I'm going to continue to find things to keep us young and relevant and most of all, interested in the world around us!

In the meanwhile, all I know is that life is short - so we eat dessert every night!

GREECE

Originally Published:

October 28, 2019

Hellas = Greece. This is the official name of our birthplace. The name Greece comes from the ancients who called it Graikos and then adapted by the Romans into Graecia. It is the land of the Hellenic people, of the Hellenistic period and the philosophy of Hellenism. Hellas, Helen, Helene (Eleni in Greek) means light. That is what strikes you when you visit Greece; the light, the sun, the brilliance of the sky is unbelievable… more so against the vivid blue of the Aegean, Ionian, and Mediterranean Seas. I like to think I was named after this luminous description, but my maternal grandmother, Eleni, would have begged to differ!

Both Zaf and I were born in Greece and to this day identify with the culture and traditions we were raised on. We had both visited Greece as teenagers and young adults; we have taken three trips there as a couple. Our experiences differ in some ways but exactly alike in numerous other aspects.

As a young adult, I visited my relatives for a short period of time and then flew/sailed off to the amazingly beautiful islands to party, party, party! Zaf, married with kids in tow, spent more time with the relatives and less on the "singles" route to memorable, swinging vacations.

We are similar though, in our feelings that in many ways, Greece is just like having another home. We are so comfortable being there – we know the language, the culture, and we know the Greeks!

Our trips to Greece we took together gave us the opportunity to explore Greece as an older couple. It is so vastly different to see a country when you are twenty-two years old versus when you are sixty-five! We wanted to see more than sunsets at the beach and the local clubs. So we have spent much time traveling by car from one end of Greece to the other. Finding off roads and discovering tiny taverns with delicious home-made food, chatting with the local people, climbing death-defying mountains through forests and gorges, entering peaceful, awe-aspiring monasteries dating back to the eleventh century, visiting castles and fortresses are only some of our shared experiences. There is so much more to see and do although we don't know where to begin!

But begin we will. Our retirement plan is to pack everything up that we want to keep, put it in storage, and take off. Using Thessaloniki as a base, we can continue to explore Greece. We also plan on using the airport there to travel and explore other parts of Europe and the Middle East. We will be there a minimum of three months, perhaps longer.

Our Greece experience, past and future, will be chronicled throughout this book for your enjoyment. You can visit Greece through our eyes, and you can add your own experiences as well. Together, we can bring more of this glorious country to light!

EXPLORE COOKING

Originally Published:

October 28, 2019

Food plays a huge role in the Greek culture. What you eat tells me who you are – and we are definitely a combination of Gyros and the All-American Burgers!

Greek cuisine, among the best in the world, is labor-intensive: the shopping, the cutting, the slicing, the chopping, the sautéing, the stirring, the spicing, and the tasting! It takes time. There is no rushing any step because it is about family and love. My mother and aunts would spend hours preparing stuffed tomatoes and peppers, pastichio, moussaka, lemon chicken and potatoes, spinach and feta cheese pies (my mother would roll out her own fillo dough!), and so many other dishes I remember from childhood.

It is not unheard of to have four-hour dinners, especially for holidays and special events. It starts with appetizers which perhaps might also be called mini meals. It is not just one or two items; it could be a plethora of tastes: feta cheese, meatballs, spinach pie bites, kalamata olives, stuffed grape-leaves, pita bread, and dips such as tzatziki and tarama.

I remember being asked, when I was a young girl, if we celebrate Thanksgiving… well duh, of course! We do it in grand style: turkey, stuffing, yams, potatoes, corn, cranberry sauce, pumpkin pies. So, does it matter if the stuffing – filled with raisins, currants, and spices – is the one my Greek dad brought over from the old country? Does it matter if the potatoes are the lemon, garlicky ones my mother perfected? Or, if the dessert table also included kataifi, melomakarona and kourambhiedes?

Alas, I have not been able to keep up with prolific output of love through cooking. Hectic days have not allowed for heavy cooking or experimenting with various new recipes. Zaf and I have settled into a weekly routine of simple meals with some barbecue items thrown into the mix. All this is about to change. I have pulled out the family recipes and earmarked the old dishes I used to cook (one learned by being attached to mother's apron) and some new ones I plan to try. This goes for desserts as well; baklava being a big challenge!

At some point, I will explore how to make a really good gazpacho, tasty guacamole, authentic Italian sauce, and a mean stir fry. There is no end to delicious food from around the world, and I intend to attempt every bit of it.

I am sure my attempts will be many; it will be wise to invest in some good digestive tablets until I get the hang of it! I will also rely on the age-old fix-it solution my mother always used: Put a little lemon on it!

Just thinking about all of this makes me eager to get going with this retirement thing. In the meanwhile, I can certainly continue exploring the foods of the world – because after all, we gotta eat!

A SINGLE ROSE

Originally Published:

October 28, 2019

My mother was just out of surgery and my sister, Tina and I, were hovering about. My brother-in-law left to go pick up dad – we had him stay home during the procedure due to his own health issues. When they arrived, Tina and I stepped back to make room for dad to get near mom; he walked slowly using his cane. Not a man of many words, he smiled, bent down, kissed her hand, and handed her a single rose. All three of us, Tina, Jerry, and I, were moved to silent tears; the nurse standing by burst into sobs. A single act of tenderness and love was demonstrated right before eyes by a very simple man who believed that actions said more than words.

What makes this event stand out to me is how I have seen and heard retired couples bark, snipe, holler, and sneer at each other, oftentimes relentlessly. At the supermarket, at the movies, at restaurants, the bickering just went on and on. Embarrassing for them and for us. You can't help but think, "Were they always this way?" Or did it begin when they retired and had nothing to do all day – they got on each other's nerves and verbalized every single "wrong" thing they felt the other was doing?

I believe that a married couple needs to stay "wed" to each other throughout the marriage – with or without kids. That the thread between the spouses was separate from any other person, related or not. That you and your spouse had a relationship with one another as one unit in thought, action and deed. Without this connection, when the kids are gone, they are left with a void…two people wandering around the house together but alone with their thoughts and memories. No wonder the bickering escalates to downright meanness and cruelty.

Retirement might just be the avenue to re-connect with one another. With time and space available, a couple can find their way back to each other. It has been said that even if you don't feel it, if you act it, the feeling will develop. Simple acts such as a pat on the hand or serving the other person first before you feed yourself can be a start. Remembering what brought you together, way back when, would be a great springboard to exploring how to return to those feelings of love and desire. Plan evenings out; it doesn't have to be fancy dinners. It could just be a burger and a beer, perhaps a movie or a play, joining a card game group, driving down to the beach or up a mountain to the pretty little inn… these are all worth exploring together as a loving couple with a shared history.

It is also time to forgive and forget… something your spouse did twenty years ago that has stuck in your craw from that day forward needs to be let go. This inner exploration of finding peace will serve all of us well. Retirement should bring us a sense of harmony and goodwill – we have earned it and should put it to good use. No need to re-hash past grievances - just explore how you can say, "I'm sorry" when necessary with what you say and do today, and then move forward.

A woman once told me that her husband brings her flowers every day. I exclaimed: EVERY DAY??? She smiled and said, "Yes…he goes out to the backyard and cuts the best ones, puts them all together in a single bouquet, and brings them to me." A daily gesture of love, commitment and tenderness!

Zaf and I will work on remembering the day we met and keeping the spark alive as we move forward into retirement. I plan to plant roses.

MEET RETIRE-AGER™ JERRY T.

Originally Published:

October 28, 2019

Meet Jerry T. He has dementia and other medical issues. Jerry's career was in the food business. Representing several companies, Jerry was on the road selling products from Europe and the Middle East. His family and close friends began seeing signs of his confusion and forgetfulness several years ago.

At first, it was dismissed as just aging, but when he got lost coming home from work several times, they realized something more was happening. He was adamant about working and would try to get into the car each morning; the family hired a driver to take him to his local clients. His boss allowed him to phase out slowly as he needed to – a grateful family appreciated his kindness. In due time and after several medical tests, the doctors verified that he did indeed have dementia. He officially retired, but the anxiety of the disease gave him sudden bursts of exclaiming, "I've got to go now; my customers are waiting."

For over forty-five years, Jerry was a hard-working man making sure that his wife and family were well taken care of – that's all he knew; that was what his focus was and what he was good at. Today, he is surrounded by family and friends to make sure he is comfortable, safe, and taken care of. Retirement was thrust upon him, he didn't willingly decide on his own. And it was the retirement he did not expect to have.

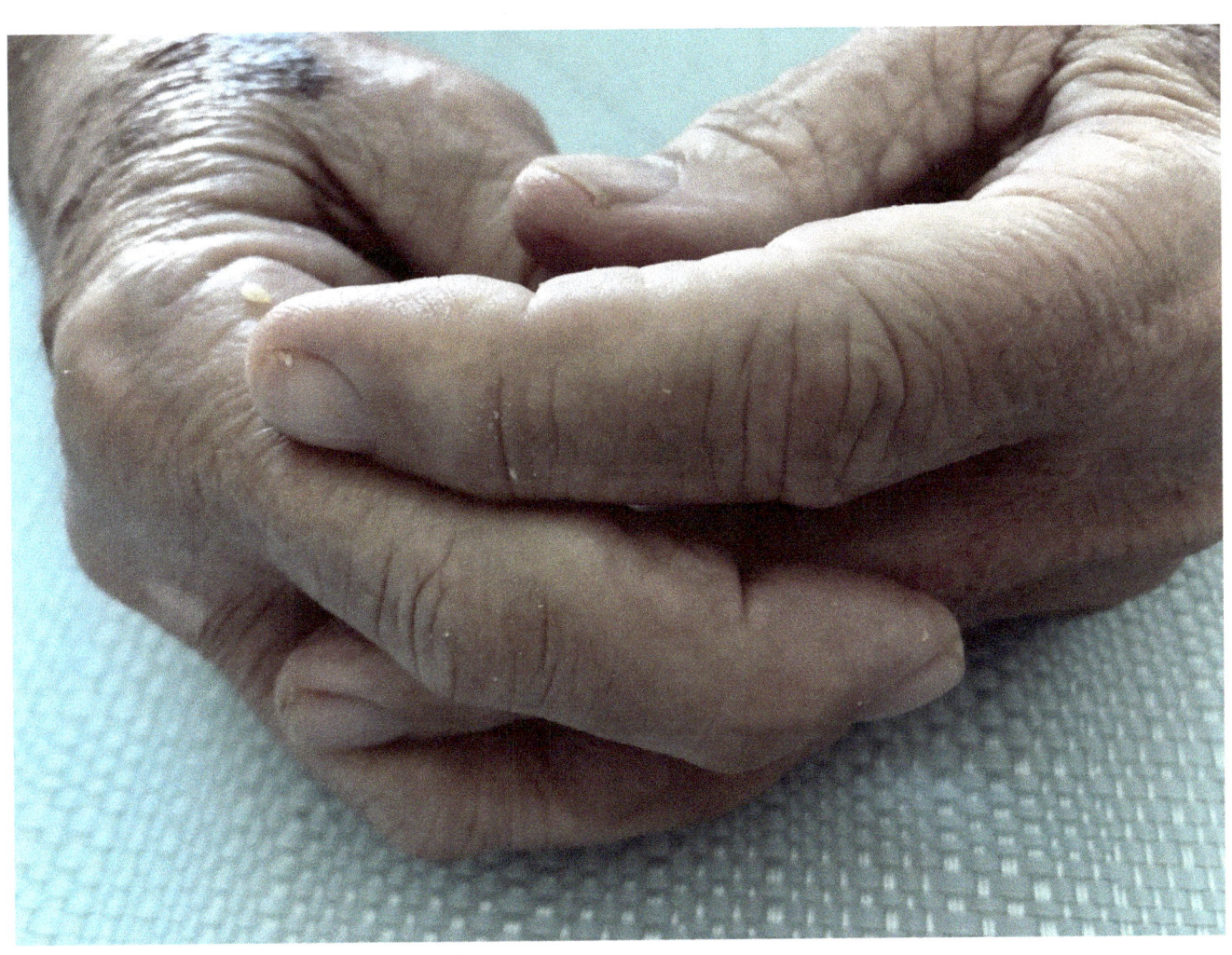

MEET RETIRE-AGER™ TINA T.

Originally Published:

October 28, 2019

Meet Tina T. Jerry's wife. A retired school teacher who had a hard time letting go of her love of teaching and the children she taught. As her husband's medical condition got worse, her children and other family members surrounded her with love and encouragement to retire and remove the stress of work and caretaking. She finally decided to do so.

It was very painful for her to lose this identity. Teaching in a neighborhood private school, she was part of a church community and was very well-known and loved. Her children all went to that school; they attended Sunday School and were active participants in all the youth activities. The whole family volunteered time, money, and effort at various events and activities. The community gave her a beautiful retirement party; she cried throughout the whole thing – especially when one student, 3000 miles away, attended the event through modern technology by Skyping and exclaiming her profound imprint on his childhood!

Tina's retirement came quickly. She had to take the measures to prepare for the unknown future with her ailing husband. They sold the house and moved into a smaller home. She became the sole caretaker of her husband. In six months, all that she knew was gone. Her husband, her job, her home. Tina was very lucky though; her new home is on the same property as her son and his family – the door is often unlocked because she got tired of getting up to open it as the kids ran back and forth between the two houses. Her friends have rallied around to make sure she gets out of the house for meals, movies, and other excursions.

For a long time, Tina resisted having other caretakers for Jerry, but now she does bring them in for a bit of respite. She has begun to create a new life for herself. Retirement was thrust upon her too and is a retirement she did not expect either.

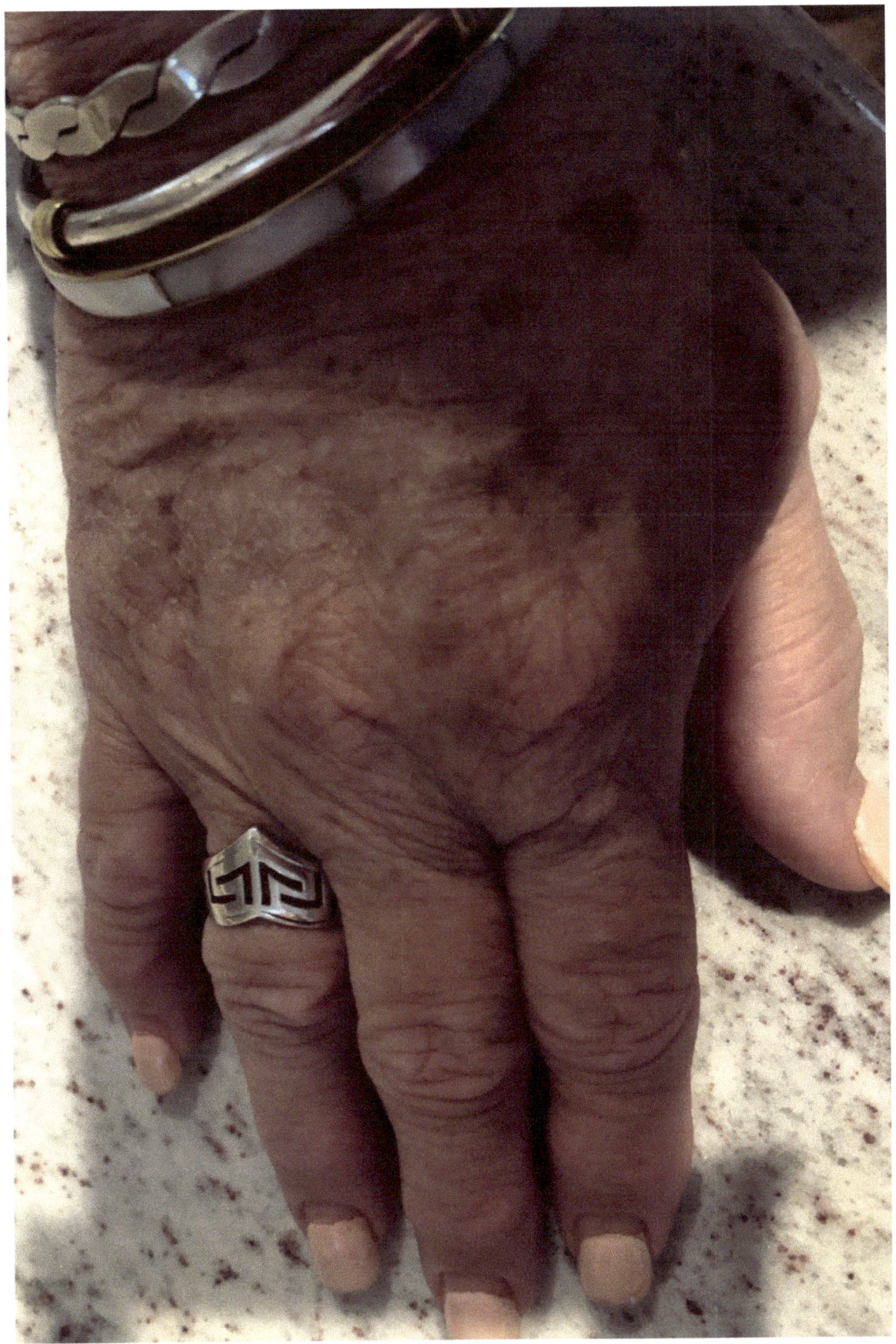

ALL THINGS ITALIAN

Originally Published:

November 22, 2019

Buon Giorno!

When I was eleven years old, I bought an Italian Dictionary. While other kids that age bought comic books and toys, my desire was to learn how to speak Italian. This was because I fell in love with Dean Martin (to this day!) and wanted to be ready to speak to him in his native tongue should I ever run into him. This turned into a life-long love of all things Italian; one of my retirement projects is to finally learn how to speak the language fluently (or at least passable). I already downloaded an app and have set a goal of a word or expression a day.

Over the years, Italy loomed large in my thoughts. I integrated the word Ciao in my every day greetings, poured over maps of Italy, and always chose Italian cuisine when eating out. The term "una faccia, una razza" speaks volumes to me. One face, one race is a shared heritage between Italy and Greece. It points out the similarities, the love of life, the zest, the energy, the passion, and the mindset of these two countries that I love. Identifying how so many words in Italian have Greek roots began as a hobby and has evolved into being a point of reference to others debating the pros and cons of each country.

My first trip to Italy was the summer between junior and senior years in college. I flew over to Florence from Athens with four friends. Naturally, I was the translator because I had taken two years of Italian and had some understanding of it, along with the absolute fervor of being there!

The second trip to Italy was after college when I worked at TWA. My parents and I planned a trip to Greece and on the way home, we stopped in Rome. It was a trip of a lifetime for them and a natural for me. We spent our days sightseeing: The Vatican, The Fountain of Trevi, The Pantheon, etc. We ate pasta and dad was amazed that I could order in Italian! We also went shopping. I remember my mother asking me "How many millions did we spend today?" The lira was still in effect then and the zeros were endless. We laughed ourselves silly imagining how wealthy we must be if we spent millions of lira!

My third trip to Italy was with Zaf – Rome, Florence and Venice. We traveled by train and had an amazing experience. Florence is my favorite – it is like walking into a work of art. I could live there and become thoroughly integrated with the lifestyle. Zaf promised a return trip to include Tuscany, Pisa, Naples, Milan, Sicily, Capri, Lake Como, Cinque Terra, and well, all of it! Once we arrive in Greece when we retire, we will plan our travels through Europe; Italy is the first place we will go!

Bravissimo!

I have gathered all my maps, books, interesting articles about places, restaurants, museums, etc. and placed them in a box marked ITALY! We are ready! The Italian dictionary is in there, too.

Exploring Italy will be the manifestation of Dolce Far Niente – the sweetness of doing nothing! Ciao bella!

PS. At our wedding, our first two dances were chosen from Dean Martin's repertoire. No one was surprised!

BOOKS AND A BELL

Originally Published:

November 22, 2019

I am primarily in charge of cleaning out our current home. We live in a home that I purchased when I was single. I had my own stuff; then my great-aunt Fanny passed on and left me all her stuff. Lots of antique, vintage furniture, dishes, glassware, and linens. Then my mother, Maria, passed on, and I shared her things with my sister. Then I met and married Zaf – once we decided it would be best for us to live here, his stuff came in too. Our garage was packed to the rafters. We had four toasters and blenders, 134 spoons, 90 glasses, over 150 dishes, and 50 towels. And that was just the everyday items; the "good" stuff was equally numerous. Beautiful to look at but hardly ever used – even for company!

Several years ago, I had to assist my sister and brother-in-law in clearing out their home to put it on the market. Due to health reasons, they were not able to do the majority of work. I spent the better part of a month going through their things: throwing out, giving away, and packing up. That's all we had: 30 days. The house sold faster than expected and the new owners wanted to move in right away. The last day was a beauty!

Even though we had a cleaning lady to go through each room and make sure it was spotless, I was a wreck. Last minute packing and moving was on a fast track coupled with the emotional side of them leaving their home. I had my hands full with their tears and sadness. Finally, it was all done; driving home – exhausted and smelly – I made a vow to the Almighty that this would not happen to me when we moved.

And so, it began. The hardest separation I had to face was with my books. As a life-long avid reader, I have accumulated over 3,500 books. All nicely placed in bookcases, on the floor, on shelves and tabletops, all over the house. I tried to sell them, but in speaking with three book buyers, they all told me that the books I owned would not fetch much. People were reading books on their computers and iPads these days. Selling them online (exploring my options!) was competitive and indeed a chore. I took a deep breath, got some boxes, and did what I call the first "pass". Textbooks and school books were the first to go – honestly, they don't do math the way we did math! Then came some books that were not as important to me - best sellers in their day but having a copy of "Valley of the Dolls" was not really necessary! I packed up 850 books and donated them to the local library. I cried a couple of times but felt a lot thinner once I got rid of this weight.

I also own about one hundred books in the Greek language: my own, my mother's, and my aunt's. Our ethnic background is Greek, so they are treasures to me. I have put my favorites aside to keep, but the bulk of them will go to the local Greek School; that makes me feel good. Bibles and other religious books will be given to our church; that makes me feel blessed.

Zaf and I went through the garage and picked out things we could let go of. Tables, chairs, clothes, filing cabinet, office supplies, etc. were packed up. I have no idea why I kept two lamps without the shades for over ten years! I then called local charities who picked up most of these items. Some things were too "used" even for them, so we had to toss them.

There was one item I could just not let go of though. My mother crocheted a beautiful table cloth, which had a stain on it I could not get out. And even though she made several of them, I could still not see myself throwing this one out. So, one day, Zaf was cleaning up his side of the garage (tools!), I placed the tablecloth on the bench and said, "I can't throw this out, so you can handle it". It was a lot easier to leave it there and walk away then to put it in a garbage bag.

Since then, I often walk around the house and eye-ball what will be in the next "pass". I have a section in the garage where I put things that will be the next to go, and we do a good job with adding to it often.

In speaking with other people who are planning to retire or have retired, we are all in agreement. The next generation does not want our things. They are not emotionally tied to them as we are. A visitor to my home may see things and say, "What is this, and why are you keeping it?" Well, that little bell shaped like a lady's ball-gown was the bell my great-aunt Fanny got in Portugal; she would give it to me to announce our family's dinner was ready when I was a little girl. Will I throw this out? – no, never. The kids and grand-kids will pick out maybe one or two items but that's about it. Whatever will I do with all the china and crystal?!

Exploring what is of value is where we are today.

TWO'S A CROWD

Originally Published:

November 25, 2019

When you marry young and are still together when you are both retired, you have plenty of time to identify each other's quirks and habits… and to get used to them (more or less). When you marry later in life, like I did, the curve for learning what makes each other tick is shorter but more intense. Either way, when you are both suddenly in the house all day, every day, it becomes a real challenge not to kill each other.

Zaf came with a household of furniture and kitchen equipment. Nothing matched my things; I painted the legs of a coffee table so it would fit in. I reframed some of his photographs to match mine. We use his glassware for cocktails and other adult beverages. The biggest concession: MY CLOSET! I had to overcome the unsettling feeling of giving up half of my space, quickly and effortlessly (ha!). I began using the second bedroom closet and bureaus so I spent much time going back and forth trying to remember where certain items are and if I still have them. When we downsize to a smaller home, who knows, my clothes may be in the garage!

Speaking of downsizing, the space we will inhabit will be smaller. Now, we can each be on either end of a long house and once in a while, I need to text him if I want to reach him. He can watch his sports while I take a nap; he can be in the office, at his desk, playing video games, and I can be reading my book in the den. Peaceful, quiet, serene. A new home that won't have the same square footage will mean that we will see each other every minute of the day in the one big central area called Open Space: kitchen, great room, dining area. Bedrooms are closer to the center of the home, and I'm hoping the doors will be soundproof!

The one area where we dance some sort is the kitchen. We both enjoy being there prepping, cooking, and most of the time, we are synchronized athletes. Other times, I have to yell out, "Coming through!" as I take a pot off the stove or a pan out of the oven and he is standing right at the exact spot I need to land, absorbed on the sports channel. He likes to place the salad bowl on the mat in the middle of the table; I need that spot to put down the hot platter. I remind him of this every time I approach the table with my hands full, and he reminds me, every time, that he cannot reach the salad comfortably when it is off to the side. We manage.

There are several projects I have lined up to do once I retire or semi-retire. Working on this blog, writing my memoir, sorting photographs, and the like. There is also the tidying up and various other household chores that need to be done. Outside the home, I plan to volunteer, take classes, visit museums and local sites I have enjoyed in the past, and explore the ones I haven't. I believe that, in general, it is easier for a woman to find things to do to keep her active and busy.

In speaking with other women whose husbands have retired, I hear a variety of experiences. One woman tells her husband what she plans on doing that day; he has the option of going with her or he can stay home. Another woman suffers in silence as she watches her husband wandering around the house and saying he is bored. A third woman gives her husband a list of things to do: fix the lamp, go to the grocery store, weed the plants, etc. Aging has its limits; one cannot work in the garden if they have a bad back. One cannot drive to the store if their vision is impaired. This dilemma impacts both parties. No one answer is right for all couples. Adjustments and compromises must be reached together.

What will Zaf be doing? Other than golf, I haven't heard him say what his other plans are. The one thing I know I can do is to make plans to go somewhere – church, the theater, lunch with friends, a drive up the coast, or a weekend further up the coast. Once I mention what I would like to do and he says yes, I buy the tickets right away so he doesn't change his mind!

Two may be a crowd, but the company we keep is special to both of us.

SCAR WARS

Originally Published:

December 04, 2019

Our friend, John, who is sitting at the head of the table on the left, gets up and walks down to Zaf who is sitting at the head of the table on the right. As he approaches, he lifts his pant leg to show his knee replacement scar. Zaf stands up and shows him his scar. Mike and Jerry, who are also seated at the table each call out: "I got one too!" The Scar Wars began! The talking becomes animated as each guy tries to share their knee-replacement experience. We women laugh at their antics. After a beat, my sister says: "Well, I had hip surgery two years ago…" and boom, we are now talking about our ailments too!

The funny thing is, as we begin to make plans to go out to dinner, someone always states, "We are not going to talk about our medical issues – we will talk about other things that make us laugh!" We all agree and hope for the best. Sometimes we are good at it, and sometimes we fall back to our old habit of discussing aches, pains, medicines, procedures, doctors, insurance, walkers, hearing aids, etc.

I told Zaf I didn't want to go out to dinner with them anymore – it's too depressing; he said ok. But he knows better. Hanging out with our crowd is a good thing as we are considered the "younger ones" even though Zaf is about the same age as the other guys. He works full time though, so he hasn't "graduated" into retirement yet. Besides, who else understands what we are going through other than our friends who are in their sixties and seventies? We are going through this stage in our lives together. Children and grandchildren are thoughtful and kind, but they are clueless as to what it means to get up in the morning and ache all over. The kisses they give us are a good remedy though!

On our recent vacation to Aruba, we were relaxing on one of the many patios of our hotel; a woman walked up to Zaf and said, "You had knee surgery?" as she pointed to his knee. Zaf said yes and she took off like a rocket about her upcoming knee surgery, her fears, her doctor's experience, pain medication, etc. While we wanted to assure her that all would be well, we couldn't get a word in! As we finally broke free, I told Zaf not to wear shorts again.

Indeed, we are on our way to being Retire-Agers™, and we have the scars to prove it. Some are visible on the outside, and some live on the inside. Some we got on our journey so far (hard-earned and well-deserved), some are newly acquired (aging), and I would venture to say there might be some in store for us in years to come (more aging!).

I find it interesting that a few people I've met try to cover up the scars while several others wear them with pride. It seems to me that this is based on how you feel about yourself. Typically, on one day, we could be confident about who we are, and the very next day, we find ourselves on the couch, the back of our wrist lying on our forehead thinking, "Who am I?" This makes us all very human.

By retirement age, we should be past this. Exploring how it would be if we didn't focus on our back twinges or our stomach discomforts would be a good way to begin. Each time I sense a throbbing sensation on my left leg (the disc is out of whack), I take my medicine and keep moving murmuring to myself, "I'm okay, I'm okay, I'm okay". Somebody once said to act a feeling until it becomes real… and so I do it. There isn't any other way to tell the tale that you are still alive and succeeding with this aging thing.

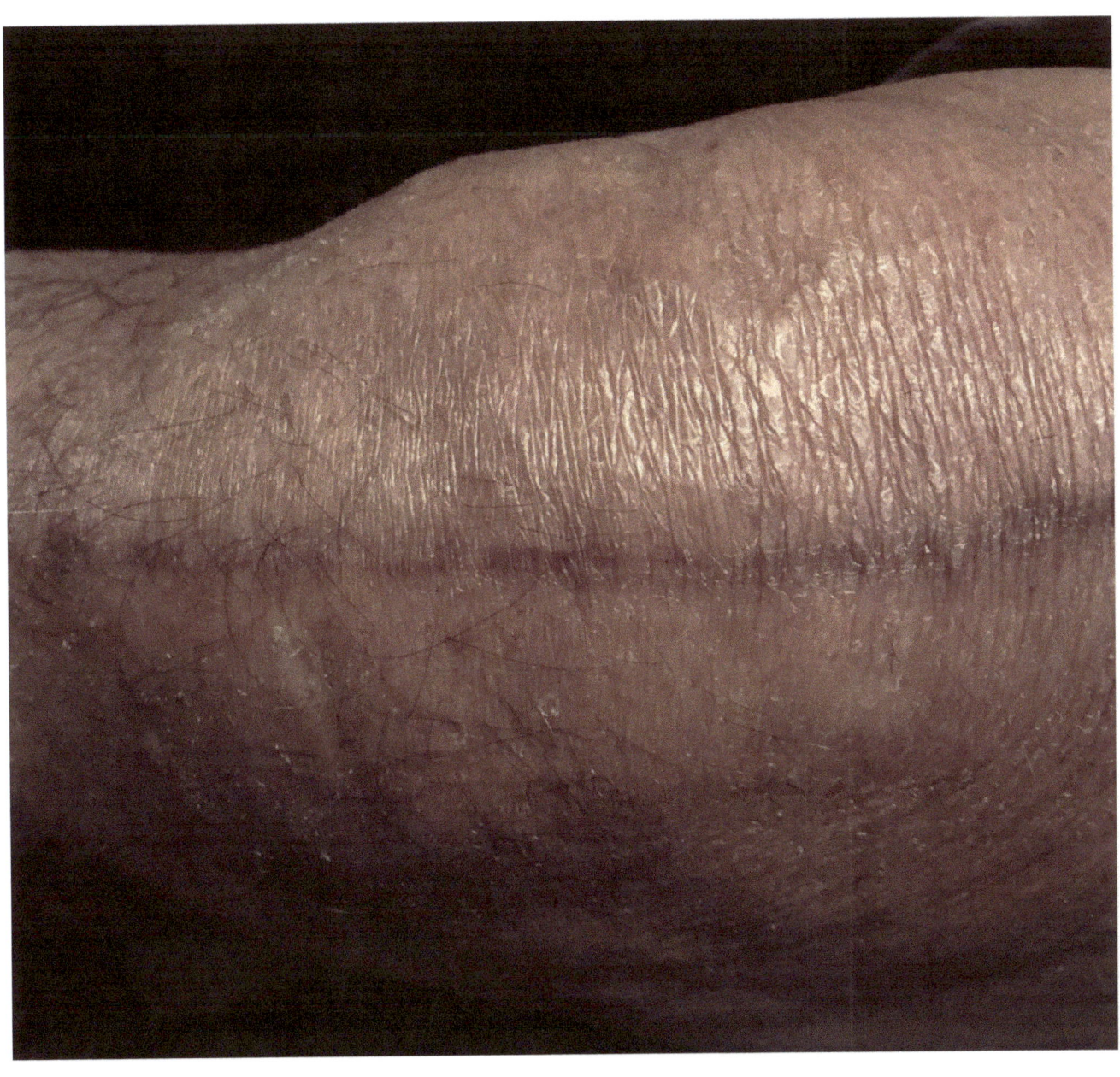

AM I GOING TO MISS THIS?

Originally Published:

December 09, 2019

I felt my stress level rise the other day contemplating how we were going to get rid of all our stuff under the label of Downsizing. Just the thought of gathering boxes, bubble wrap, packing tape, scissors, and the energy... then going through the closets and the garage (oh my!) and deciding what goes and what stays was giving me a panic attack. Not only are our clothes in our bedroom closet, but the guest bedroom closet, two dressers, and two bedside cabinets have the "overflow." Granted, a lot of them we don't wear very often, but still, I gotta make some decisions here.

And then we have the furniture, the pictures, and the what-nots all over the house which I have loved and taken care of all these years. Looking at 80% of my house, I see my mother and my aunt whose things have lived with me for over twenty years in my own home. They have lived with me for over fifty years as I was growing up in their homes. The shelves and credenzas hold my memories. The artwork and pictures reflect our family, our heritage, and our travels.

My mind was working overtime thinking, "What if I get rid of something and then regret it or realize I made a mistake? How will I feel? Will I cry? Will the rest of my family still speak to me while I'm crying?"

I shared this with the two people I am the closest to... and they both thought I was nuts. My husband Zaf has no problem with tossing something out when he's "done" with it. My sister Tina went through an entire household dismantling several years ago (for medical reasons) where virtually nothing was kept except clothes, pictures, and the good china. She now told me, "I miss nothing; I have all that I need in my new home with new things that make me happy!" Drat! I thought she of all people would understand since I watched the tears flow down her cheeks when the moving company drove away from their home. But now, three years later, she's Pollyanna.

The good news is that I found a way to honor my books. I am re-reading them and when done, they go into the box in the garage to be donated to the library. The bad news is whether or not I can put the book in the box!

While I'm busy with my work and maintaining the home, in the back of my mind is the burden of, "I've got to get started." I've earmarked January 2020 to begin listing items for sale on all online sites I know of and maybe finding a few more. Someone gave me a piece of contact information on good estate sale people, but I'm hesitant to do this. We tried it for my sister and brother-in-law; it was a fiasco. People strolling through the house – we had to have a staff person in every room, so nobody got light-fingered. We went through all that effort to lay things out and only a handful of people showed up. We should have spent the energy and time to just pack things up in the first place. A glorified garage sale was what it was, so we'll see.

I would prefer to spend my brain power on exploring what I want our retirement to look like, but the priority is to explore how we're going to get there. And put that into action. That is where I'm at today. Wish me luck!

SURPRISE!

Originally Published:

January 11, 2020

One of the pleasures of meeting someone new is discovering the layers of their personality and being astonished!

My husband Zaf is the reserved type. Having a Greek background, one would assume that he was animated and full of zest! But, he's not. Tall, dark, and handsome, yes...but inner strength, wisdom, and dignity make up his true character and personality. It is a perfect balance for me who is lively, energetic, and perky!

At first, we enjoyed getting to know each other over dinner, long drives along the beautiful California coast, and sharing our dreams. As we progressed in our relationship, we learned how much alike we are in thought, actions, and beliefs. Our joy increased with all these discoveries and realized very quickly that we were a match!

And then one day, he asked me to follow him to the garage. Right there, off to the side, under a cover was a Harley motorcycle! I was speechless – which doesn't happen very often as family and friends would tell you. He was so excited. He was so proud. He was so eager for me to join him on a ride! Stunned, amazed, and astonished... that doesn't even begin to describe what I was feeling at that moment.

He had it all planned... he provided my helmet, gloves, and scarf. He made sure I had sturdy shoes, a leather jacket, and goggles. He mapped out the route of our first excursion. He laughed when I hesitated and assured me that I would be safe. A brand new personality emerged with this new adventure he wanted to take me on. **Surprise!** So, what is a girl supposed to do? I said a quick prayer and jumped on.

To simply say that I was terrified is not enough. I did not let go of his black leather jacket. I clutched his middle with every ounce of strength I had, keeping my eyes shut all the way. He chose an easy road to get started on, but soon we entered Cleveland National Forest in Orange County, CA, where we twisted and turned as the road meandered through hills and curves.

Eventually, I peeked open one eye and then the other. I relaxed a bit and breathed a little easier. We encountered other riders, and I saw how they greeted each other as they rode by. I did not realize that the way they said hello was to lay their arm along the side of the bike and point downwards. I waved at them like I was the Queen of England! While I did not hear it, I saw their laughter!

Exploring the Southern California mountains, beaches, and countryside was soon the norm; the best part was seeing Zaf so happy that we were exploring places together. But as it does happen often, good things sometimes come to an end. Work and other obligations prevented us from going out on the bike for months at a time. When Zaf retired from his first job, he would go out alone. I went off to work with the cell phone glued to my ear… so afraid that I would get a call with not-so-good news. My anxiety increased to the point where I demanded that he call me every hour no matter where he was and even if he had to get off the bike to do so. Before long, he would come home a bit tired and spent. He did not go riding that often. I sent a secret Thank You! to the heavens above.

It was decision time. Keeping it was a temptation; it was a reminder of times past. But it was taking up so much room in the garage! This was a sensitive issue. I could not say get rid of it – that you are too old, that you were not strong enough to handle it, etc. So, I waited for him to realize this on his own.

Finally, at dinner one night, he told me that the last time he went out for a ride, other riders coming up behind him on a mountain road had to pass him because he was going too slow. He found himself unable to keep up. He did not feel strong enough to do what he needed to do to stay safe, so he sold the bike. I commiserated with him and assured him that we would find other ways to explore the world. He sold the bike – we went on a cruise!

The aging process brings an end in one way but opens in another. The key is not to remove but to replace. Not doing so brings depression and a sense of uselessness. Thoughts become narrow and isolated. Hopelessness creeps in. We need to be on alert – something new and wonderful just might happen, and we need to be ready for it!

WHICH ONE WILL I BE?

Originally Published:

January 13. 2020

At the market last week, I saw one register lane wide open, so I slid right in and unloaded my groceries. The woman in front of me was pulling out her wallet so I knew I didn't have a long wait. At a closer look, I noticed that she was about 80 years old; I sighed inwardly because she was fumbling and could not get her credit card out. She finally got it and inserted it into the machine; it was declined. The clerk said to try again; she did, to no avail. She pulled out another card, and the same thing happened. Clutched in her left hand, I saw that she had at least another six or seven cards and some of them still had activation stickers on them. She then pulled out her wallet and began to write out a check. The people lined up behind me, and we all waited. The clerk asked for ID; she handed over her driver's license. Upon inspection, he could not use it as it was expired. She was flustered. The manager comes over and tells her that she needs to renew her license and suddenly the woman remembered that she did and had her paperwork in her purse. Case solved… we moved on. I couldn't help but think how sad this was that no one was with her to assist – a child, a grandchild, a caretaker. She pushed her filled cart out the door and shuffled off to the parking lot all alone.

The next time I went to the market, another eighty-year-old woman was in front of me. This one though, was alert, quick, and pleasant… she worked the credit card payment process easily and quickly exchanged smiles with the clerk, loaded up her walker seat, and off she went at a good pace.

I remember yet another experience at the market from a few years ago. As I walked towards the market, I heard a voice calling out, "Miss, can you help me?" I looked over to the side and saw an old woman pushing her cart, purse dangling from the crook of her arm which was shaking and shuffling. I ran over, and she said, "Please help me to my car." I took hold of her cart – thank goodness the drivers of the three cars in the immediate area saw what was happening and they all stopped. I tried to steer her down the incline. She would not let go, and she would not move. Another woman came over to help me help her. I told her I would take her hands off the cart and hold her up while I took the cart. The old woman gave me a struggle – she said, "Don't take my purse." I assured her I would not, took a strong hold of her, and walked her down to the car. She found her keys, I opened the door, and got her settled. The other woman opened the passenger side of the car and loaded up a few groceries. I asked the old lady if there was anyone I could call for her; she said there wasn't. I waited until she caught her breath and felt strong enough to drive. I said goodbye and a silent prayer.

A friend is 85 years old – she lives alone with her three cats and has a part-time caretaker… she handles her own banking and finances. Upon the recent sale of her million-dollar home, she moved into something a bit smaller on one level. She was driving until she was 83 and only gave it up because she now needs to cart an oxygen tank around, and that is a bit too much. Talking to her is a delight – she has had such an interesting life filled with ups and downs… she is sharp, quick, and witty.

Two women in my Greek community are 99 ½ years old and 100 years old respectively. They are sharp as a tack; they walk (slowly), they remember who I am (most of the time!), they ask questions (how are you dear?), and ask that I say hello to Zaf! Role models, indeed.

Guess who I want to be? The differences between these women are astounding. What makes them so different? Is it the life they led when they were younger? Is it a mindset? Is it a medical or physical illness? Is it genetics? I don't know. I wish I did; I would wave a magic wand and give this blessing to everyone.

I push myself every day to get some exercise - both physical and mental. As an early riser, I am at my desk by 6:00am, coffee in hand, checking my e-mails and responding to students (I teach several online courses) and clients. I check the bank balances and pay bills. Most importantly, I blog. Household chores are next with a thought to what's for dinner. Washed and dressed, I run errands or meet with clients. I take a power nap that gives me the oomph I need to do other things as needed for the balance of the day and evening. Zaf comes home, we have dinner, and find our way to the couch for some TV watching.

This is the life I'm living right now. I take each day as it comes and pace myself, trying not to think about the sorting, purging, and packing that needs to be done for our big move! One day, it will all be done, and we will be on our way to becoming Retire-Agers™!

DOUBLE THE FUN

Originally Published:

January 27, 2020

Most of my early travels were done when I was single. So many of my girlfriends were doing what I was doing: living alone, following a career path, seeking a relationship, and building a life with what we had, which included trips here and there.

A good friend I spent an enormous amount of time back home turned into a brand new person when I traveled with her! I am sure she felt the same way about me. Living 24/7 with someone is vastly different from spurts of shared outings, dinners out, bar hopping, and crying on their shoulder. Little things that were a bit annoying at the beginning became bigger obstacles when you are a plane ride away from home! With time, you gain patience, perspective, and most of my friendships survived.

Deciding where to go was the first task. Domestic? International? Fly or drive? The beach, mountains, camping, Vegas? I'm not a beach person; I burn easily and get bored easily. Spending five days lying on a beach towel is not my idea of fun. I don't ski or hike – I am more of a lodger with a toddy type of person. While I do dabble at the slots, I don't make large bets; I have a drink or two but do not get sloshed. Camping??? Heck no…using up one day to pack everything up so I can spend another day unpacking is the first no-no; doing my cooking and cleaning while on vacation is the second one. There are more reasons why I don't camp, but I won't go into them!

I like touring towns and cities to see how people live; I enjoy walking through neighborhoods and exploring shops, village squares, museums, cafes, etc. Some of my best experiences include trying to communicate with the locals when we didn't speak a common language. On my first trip to Paris over thirty years ago, when I was buying croissants, trinkets, clothes, etc., I took a different approach. The conversion rate from dollar to franc was confusing to me. I would put money in my hand, offer it to the salesperson, and smile. They smiled back, shrugged, and took the amount they needed. Back at the hotel, I would slowly do the calculation and am happy to report I was never cheated.

Planning on when we go and for how long became an issue as everyone has a different vacation schedule and budget. We may have had the time for a longer trip but that equated to more hotel, food, and site-seeing expenses; everyone had a different wallet size which made it difficult to agree on a trip that was comfortable for all.

Along came Zaf. We fit in well together, right from the start. As we planned our early trips, apprehension loomed. They say that you don't know someone well enough until you travel with them… and they are right! For the most part, we were okay. Directions seem to be the biggest issue. Turn left, turn right, go straight were often disagreed upon, and we often found that long stretches of silence filled the car when I, looking at a map, I'd say right, and he went left! Curiously enough, this still happens!

I made an interesting and important discovery on one trip. While walking about and exploring a city, we typically bring a small bag to carry shopping, sweaters, bottles of water, etc. At times, it would become quite bulky and heavy so I would try to pass it off to Zaf to carry. He had a really hard time with that on one trip. Not because he didn't want to. He just didn't want to carry a pink bag! I bought a navy blue bag at the nearest shop, moved the items from the pink bag into it, and Voila! He was comfortable, and boy, was I comfortable too!

Having someone you love alongside you as you explore new worlds is double the fun. You experience it at the same time, and you talk about it later, for years to come. You look through the pictures together, reminisce, and re-live it as though you were just there. The fun increases when I remember it one way, and he has a different memory. Was it our first trip to Greece when we met the bikers on the bus? Was it our first trip to Florida when we went through the Everglades? Each time we try to remember, I drag out the pictures, look at the dates, and double-check!

Our first fun trip to Greece, the challenge was on! We planned to visit our respective "villages" from where our families came from. We had a contest going – which was the best village? We went to mine first – high in the mountains of Central Greece, tucked under enormous trees along a streaming creek with picturesque bridges; it close to a historic monastery reached by a treacherous curving mountain road. He liked it right away and said, "You win!" I was surprised he gave in so easily, way before we got to his village. Once we got there, I realized why. His village is like a tiny town; the borders on all sides connect to other tiny towns, so they are all connected into one big area. Not like a village at all. It is charming though and holds many cherished memories for Zaf and me.

The retirement plan we have in mind is to see more of the world, to explore places we have never been to, and to bring home more cherished memories.

WE ARE EVERYWHERE!

Originally Published:

February 03, 2020

Within the hour, after checking in at our hotel in Lihui, Hawaii, we met two couples that are retired. Our rooms were not ready, so we all lingered over snacks, drinks, and conversation. After the initial greetings, we dove into our questions about where they were from and how their retirement began… When did you retire? Why did you retire? How are you spending your time (other than traveling to Hawaii!)?

"It was time." "I wasn't planning to, but my husband did and he wanted to travel and do other things. Health issue was looming, so we said, "Let's be good to ourselves." What are we waiting for?" All these answers seem to be universal in the world of retirement. After these points were made, the dialogue moved into example after example of people they knew of who postponed retiring because: "They really need me here so I don't feel I should go." "I don't know what I'm going to do with myself." "I want to make a bit more money so I can really enjoy myself." And yet, in each case, sadly, they never got to retire because illness prevented it, and/or they passed on. Our new poolside friends are on a quest to get the most out of retirement – yay for them!

We were a bit surprised to see so many Retire-Agers™ here. Of course, it is a more serene environment than Maui or Oahu, where the younger people gather to party, party, party. And of course, it is post-holidays and pre-spring break, so school is in session. But the number of us in our age group is far more evident than any other. This beautiful isle is the perfect destination for Retire-Agers™ to gather, relax, and meet up with others doing the same thing. I love to watch them… in the pool doing exercises, taking a swim in the warm water of the Pacific, going for a long walk, or heading to the golf course. The hotel offers a full schedule of activities: yoga, ukulele lessons, joint massages, garden tours, learning simple Hawaiian words and phrases, painting and other crafts, tours to the state park, and other points of interest, etc.…and they are lining up at the door to get in! I also like to watch them at meal times where they settle in and begin their animated conversations. These people are adamant about exploring and living life; I admire them. I plan to emulate them to the best of my ability. By far, the best thing I like to do is talk to them! I find their stories fascinating – it was history in the making, and everyone played a part. The word history, in Greek, is Istoria. It means both history AND story – because after all, it is one and the same. These people are living proof of it.

After dinner, we chatted up another couple sitting at the bar next to us. They are Retire-Agers™ and are enjoying life – they are energetic, youthful, and fun! They told us they have always wanted to visit Greece – specifically, the island of Santorini. I whipped out my phone and showed them the photos I had of this beautiful place. That clinched it… they will try to get there next year when we are there so we can show them the Greek ropes!

Retire-Agers™ are everywhere! I am not sure if that is because we are of the same age so we naturally gravitate toward one another, or if there are so many of us now that we have taken over… what do you think?

I've told everyone we met so far (three couples in one day!) about my blog and hope they tune in…. there is so much more to come!

14 OUT OF 18

Originally Published:

February 7, 2020

As we were strolling back from dinner the other night, Zaf sighed and mumbled, "Boy, this aging thing takes a lot out of you." This admission is slow in coming as my husband is highly motivated to keep "this aging thing" at bay as long as possible. He works a full-time job and commutes about an hour in each direction; on the weekends, he also oversees another business that we own. He also does a good amount of chores around the house; two weeks ago, he climbed to the rooftop to pull lemons off the tree! So, this acknowledgment of growing old was indeed rare.

The day before, he had a series of cramps in various parts of his body. He gets them often, mostly at night. This is something to discuss with the doctor should he ever get around to making an appointment. They eventually passed, and he went to sleep. The next morning after breakfast, he went out to play golf. He said he felt fine, but I told him he has to stay out of the sun, drink lots of water, and call me, 911, or the golf office ASAP should he feel bad. He scoffed but promised to do so. He informed me all went well as he stumbled in several hours later, exhausted and dehydrated. Clever me, I had purchased water and sports drinks earlier that day as I tried not to worry too much about his well-being.

We both have our share of aches and pains. Zaf had a full knee replacement about a year ago (reference SCAR WARS) and from time to time, I see him rub the area as if to soothe it. He has allergies, his stomach gets upset often, and his calves hurt. He has high blood pressure. I have high cholesterol. The disc issue on my lower back (left side) is ongoing as the pain shoots down the entire leg, my acid reflex plays havoc with my eating choices, arthritis makes an entrance often, and we both can stand to lose a few pounds. But otherwise, we're good!

Much healthier than the previous generation at the same age, we are much more active and alert; we have the drive to keep moving forward and not succumb to the lure of the comfortable chairs in front of the TV and call it Life. And yet, I can't help remembering my mother, specifically, as she rubbed ointments of one kind or another to help with her arthritis pain. We do, indeed, take different medicines than our parents did, but we take them nevertheless.

	6	7	8	9	OUT	Int	10	11	12	13	14	15	16	17	18	IN
	19	384	169	459	3655		571	443	367	474	210	473	331	173	459	3501
					2488		531	387	362	437	192					
							491	377	334	411	170	399	265	134	402	2983
							4	16	18	6	8	10	14	12	2	
													3	4		35

We settled into cozy chairs in front of the fireplace on the hotel property after our stroll. I was ready to begin: "Well honey, after we retire, we will need to find other activities that aren't…..". But just then, a young couple sitting next to us introduced themselves and we began to chat. They asked us about any other travel we have done and Zaf began with stories about Alaska, Russia, Budapest, Berlin, Italy, and of course, Greece. They were astounded and said how fortunate we are (and continue to be) as we outlined our retirement plans. They expressed much joy for us… and we for them.

So instead of a pep talk, I shared how much we have done so far - with our businesses, our travels, and how we manage to do them both. He agreed as we held hands on the way back to our room. I couldn't help to think that playing 14 holes out of 18 was an accomplishment to be proud of!

ONE FELL SWOOP

Originally Published:

February 14, 2020

"Waist level," said the woman to the contractor as she was remodeling her kitchen. No more bending to reach the pot in the back of the bottom cabinet or stretching to get the pitcher on the top shelf. I agree.

Being good to ourselves is a must for us now. We have to watch where we step, how we turn, how we sit, etc. to be safe; it represents at least one measure of control of our actions.

As Zaf and I are beginning to move things out of the house toward our goal of downsizing, it allows us to move the things we will keep into a better position to allow for easier movements and accessibility. There really is no reason to have a multitude of soaps, shampoo, lotions, etc. in the cabinet; one would think there will be a worldwide shortage, so we need to store them up! We are using them up as fast as we can! Chairs, tables, and other odds-and-ends that won't make the cut for the move are being sold/donated. It is amazing how simple and safer our actions can be once we remove the clutter!

Dropping things is a challenge with my lower back pain. A deep breath is taken as I bend carefully to pick it up. If it rolls under the bed or a bureau, the broom comes out and is put to good use.

A while ago, I made a disparaging remark about pants with an elastic band at the waist. After a beat, my older sister says, "What's wrong with them?" Duh – she was wearing them. I gulped and tried to make amends. And now… well, I saw a cute pair the other day when I was out shopping…but I resisted. One day soon, though, and they will be mine!

There is a wealth of comfortable, fashionable clothes for us Retire-Agers™ in stores and online. Given the percentage of the population in our age group, we are a hot market. I like the longer tops in particular (don't you just hate those short ones that cover nothing but your shoulders?!). Sweaters have bigger buttons for those arthritic hands. Shoes have Velcro closings – just like the ones for toddlers – and what a joy they are to get in and out of. We can still look attractive and age-appropriate with all the options out there; we can still be "cool" (not dowdy); we can still be stylish (not boring); we can still be Retire-Agers™ (not old people)! I just love exploring this new clothes thing!

Over the past months, I developed a system when changing clothes. Pants, underwear, and socks come off all in one movement. Since pulling things down requires a bending motion, why not? I call it: One Fell Swoop!

TAKE A BOW!

Originally Published:

February 21, 2020

CONGRATULATIONS! JOB WELL DONE!

We have reached the retirement milestone, one way or another, and we have the memories, the photographs, the scars to prove it!   Here's what we did:

Raised children, cooked, cleaned the house, did the laundry.

Tended to ill parents/spouse/relative.

Worked 9 – 9 in an office, store, factory, farm, etc.

Started/managed/ran a business.

Fought in wars; protested wars; lived through wars.

Screamed over Sinatra, Elvis and The Beatles.

Use a key to tighten our roller skates.

Applauded the moon landing.

Bought tools at Sears.

Wore fringed vests.

Saluted the casket pulled by a rider-less horse

Played stickball and hopscotch on the street in front our house.

Did the Lindy, the Stroll, the Locomotion, the Hand-jive, the Wahtusi and the Mashed Potatoes.

Dropped out, tuned out and found Nirvana.

Tasted our first frozen dinner.

Shaped our hair into a beehive.

Laughed at Lucy stomping grapes and nodded when Opie got words of wisdom from his dad, Sheriff Andy.

Read all about Archie, Veronica, Betty, Reggie and Jughead.

Made a phone call with a dime.

Rock N' Rolled

Vee'd the Peace Sign.

Heard the tinkling of the milk bottles being delivered to the front door.

Visited Peyton Place.

Harmonized in four-parts.

Owned a hula hoop.

Put flowers in our hair.

Loved Edith Bunker.

Tried to understand Wifi.

Motowned

Passed hand-me downs to younger siblings or wore one ourselves.

Had coffee in a local coffee shop, not a chain.

Marched for Civil Rights.

Tuned into American Bandstand.

Mourned Marilyn.

Read a real book and enjoyed turning the pages.

Shopped at Woolworth's.

Sat on fire-escapes on hot, summer nights.

Forced to wear a snow suit over our Halloween costume.

Watched Howdy Doody, Captain Kangaroo and The Three Stooges.

Donned a Nehru jacket.

Hung love beads around our neck.

Twisted the night away.

Set the Mini skirt trend.

Recycled, repurposed, refinanced, reprogrammed, RETIRED!

Survived the 60's, muddled through the 70's, worked through the 80's, connected online in the 90's, explored retirement in the 2000's and beyond!

We're on it!

TURN THE PAGE

Originally Published:

February 28, 2020

Don't you just hate it when a memory of how someone hurt you comes back to haunt you time and time again? It lies dormant on the back burner of your brain, and boom, it emerges loud and clear as though it happened yesterday. It quickly becomes like a movie reel, playing those old movies that should have been left in the can. With all this new-found leisure time in retirement, thinking about the past is a common, popular trend from what I hear.

It happens to me (and I'm not even retired!) now and then when triggered by a photo - something someone said or did, something I read or see. I hate it when that happens! It brings back that old hurt feeling and puts me in a bad mood, so I've got to spend the time and effort to get back to being okay with myself.

The recollection of these hurtful moments for me includes an ex-fiancé in college who broke my heart, a boss who talked about me in front of her friends (it was so obvious!) in another language as they all laughed (not allowing me to defend myself as she spoke English fluently), the guy at the supermarket who screamed at me for having coupons (I did wait in line behind other people who had coupons!), a relative who told my mother and me that I was not dressed appropriately in that mini-skirt, the teacher who talked down to my immigrant parents, a friend who dated my boyfriend (and that boyfriend who dated my friend), the man who kept slamming the tray behind my airplane seat and the airline crew that did nothing about it, the boyfriend's mother who snubbed me cause I wasn't rich enough, the part I didn't get in a play because I wasn't "hanging out" with the director, and all those times that I never spoke up for myself when I should have.

I've got some work to do on stopping that thought process; it's like a hang-nail that you can't stop picking. When I start those scenes in my head, I try to force myself to go in another direction. I say WRITE! From there, I began to think of blog ideas about how we are preparing to retire and what is on our list of what to do when we retire to keep busy and active.

Letting go is a two-step process. Forgiving those people who behaved badly is the first step to forgetting, which is the second step. After all, their conduct was more telling about who they were as people than anything else. They and the re-hashing of these negative experiences have taken up space in my mind, for free, for decades. I need that space to be able to fill it with new memories as we explore new activities, new travel, and new friends.

The upcoming chapters will lead to the grand finale of a life well-lived. I've got to get through those chapters to see how it all turns out… and to do that, I've got to get away from the past chapters and turn the page.

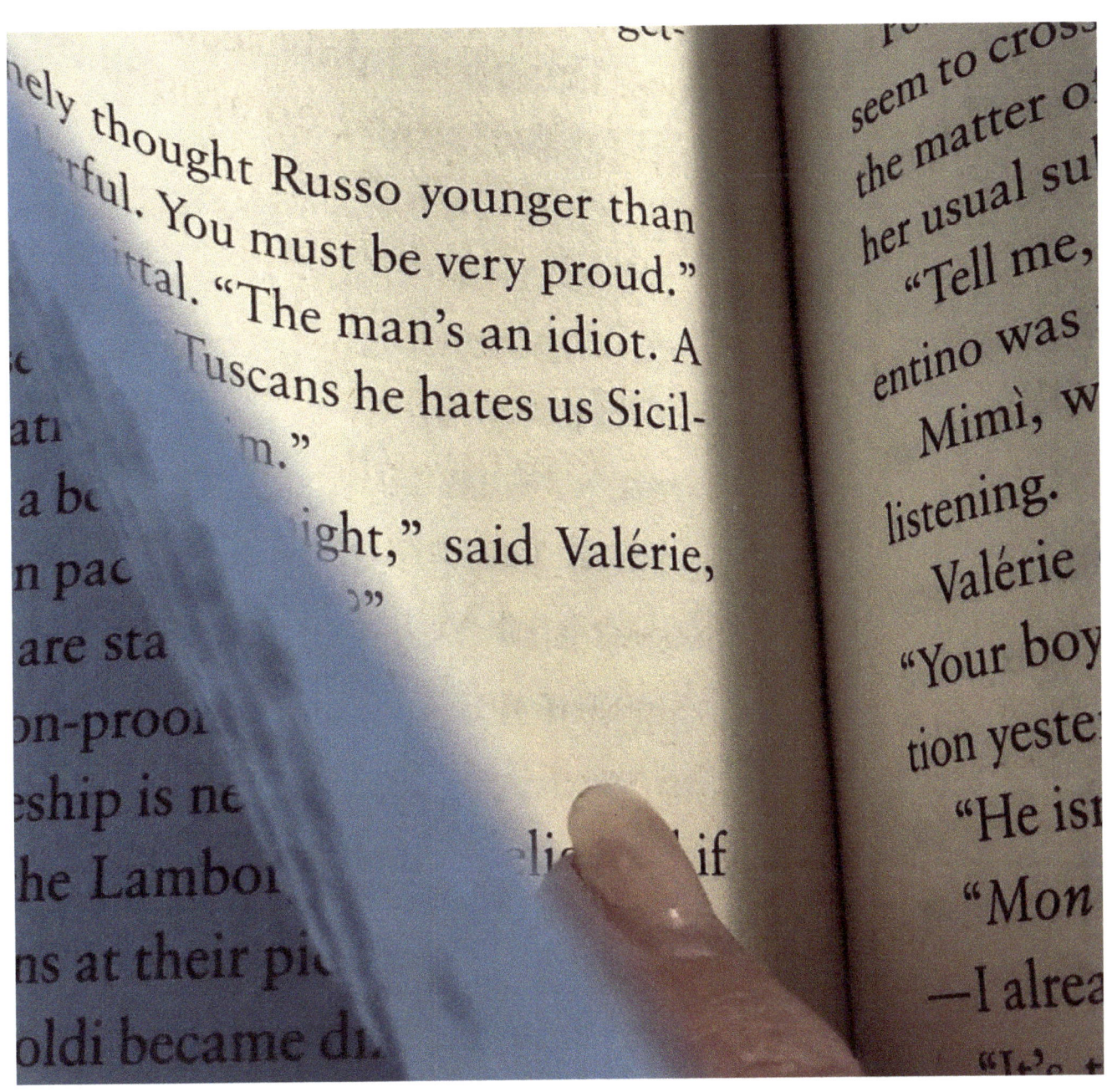

YOU STILL WEARING THAT?

Originally Published:

March 16, 2020

Pointing her finger at my faded blue shirt, my sister shrieked, "You're still wearing that?!" I stammered out, "Obviously I am." She rolled her eyes; only an older sister who has been with you since birth would have an intimate knowledge of your wardrobe.

Her comment was stuck in my head all day, and I finally concluded that since I was exploring retirement by downsizing, re-locating, etc. my clothes should be part of it. I walked into the closet and there they were: the offending garments that I've had for forever. I tried some on – but it was no use – they had to go. Empty hangers were then waiting for the new me.

Clothes do not define a person – we all know that – but what we wear does make a statement. I know of a woman in her early seventies; she dresses like a pre-teen and looks ridiculous. There is such a thing as "trying too hard" which fools no one but yourself. I know an 83-year-old woman who dresses in cool and hip outfits – with a hat to match and fun jewelry… Go Ethel B.!

I love the leggings and a long tunic look. It covers my tush, makes me look thinner and taller, and is comfortable to move around in. I can dress it up or down as I need to. Leggings can't be too tight for me though – they make my legs look like a leg of lamb! My preference is gauzy or light cotton clothes that seem to float around my body and can be layered in multiple ways.

Women are not the only ones who are apparel-challenged. Men have this issue too. Short, spandex pants are often too tight and really, are they necessary to wear to the market or dinner? Do we need to see everything?

And then we have the ragamuffins… the ones that throw clothes on simply to cover themselves. Often mismatched, pants dragging on the ground, hair unkempt. It is as though they have given up caring about themselves. Or, perhaps a touch of dementia? Perhaps that's all they have or can't afford to buy new ones? It is sad to see this.

We are not our grandmothers or even our mothers, who in middle age were considered old by society and indeed thought of themselves as old. Most dressed the part. I remember my dad bringing home a pair of shorts for my mother to wear; she wore them around the house to get used to them and cried throughout the entire day. My dad took them back. A house dress and slippers were the norm for indoor wear. Our neighbor wore nylons rolled to the top of her knee! The women of my era dressed the part with old lady underwear and sensible shoes. And always a sweater over everything. TGWANT – Thank Goodness We Are Not Them!

The good news is that there is so much to choose from – entire magazines dedicated to us. Stores and online sites abound at all price levels. We don't have to be dowdy or frumpy; we can create a look for ourselves that exudes energy, vivacity, strength, and fun! We can wear skirts and pants, shawls and capes, all types of hats and scarves, shoes, sandals and boots, dangling earrings and dazzling bracelets, and carry large bags and satchels. Our haircuts can be sophisticated and modern (and easy to care for), we can get facials and massages, and our fingernails can match our toes! The possibilities are endless when we begin to explore. And we look fabulous!

As a generation, we are so much younger in looking, feeling, and thinking than our ancestors. Fighting time is not our issue – we are having the time of our lives!

PS. The old things I am keeping are my mother's short, pink, soft cotton pajama top, my father's blue sweater, and my aunt's Christmas sweater – black with red and green appliques; these items bring me comfort.

NATURE'S BEAUTY

Originally Published:

March 30, 2020

▬▬▬

DATE/TIME: March 2020 – We are living in an eerily strange time. A virus has pushed us into a life nobody predicted or asked for. A life fraught with uncertainty, anxiety, and fear. Some have lost loved ones, some are paralyzed with worry, and some are wallowing in despair.

And yet, so many of us have hope and courage. Those of us who have lived through times such as this through wars, depressions, poverty, and hunger know that all things have a beginning and an end. "This Too Shall Pass" is a mantra we hear repeatedly, as we believe it in our hearts and share it with others via social media.

Physical distancing has not prevented us from joining a community of family, friends, and virtual strangers to encourage, soothe, and hearten our concerns and apprehensions. Our online connections are filled with inspiring quotes, humorous pictures, and creative ideas on how to stay busy as we re-discover our homes.

Animated suspension is how I describe my tenure of staying home. Although I have worked from home for over thirty years and am comfortable with being at home for lengths of time, this newfound time of not being able to leave the home at will has allowed for more inspection of how to downsize for the retirement future we have planned and still anticipate despite the transformations we are currently experiencing.

Boxes of books and household items are stacked up in the garage. Just before this crisis reached epidemic proportions, I planned to visit the library and the donation centers. Until I do that, I don't have room in there to add more items. People and companies I want to call to get quotes and estimates for the repairs needed and services I will need to make our move are not working right now. I want to do more but am at a standstill.

As I sit at my desk and do a bit of work (yes, I am blessed to have this online option!) and do my share of social media posts, I have the curtain open to the world. On warm days, I open the sliding door and breathe the fresh air as I give up a word of thanks. I look around and am grateful that nature's beauty still surrounds me.

And yet, human nature is the most beautiful – kindness, sacrifice, and compassion abound with those we see on the media who aid others in this time of unease, tension, and apprehension. They rightly call them heroes – I call them people because deep down that is how I truly believe we are made.

May the Beauty of Nature, in all forms, surround you forever and for a day.

PERFECT TIMING

Originally Published:

April 10, 2020

"Whatever happened to….?" It seems like all at once we began asking this question… right about the age of 50, we suddenly developed the need to know about people we haven't thought about in decades.

Perhaps we find some old photographs, run into an old friend, or get an invitation to attend a reunion; whatever the trigger is, we then begin the search for answers of what became of "Bob – your high school debate partner" or "Mrs. Henderson – your 2nd-grade teacher" or "Mr. Gomez – the kind next door neighbor in apartment B?

My cousin is one of those people who remembers everybody. She has kept up with them and if they are no longer with us, she knows their children and grandchildren. She often tells me, for example, that she spoke with Mary, who is the daughter-in-law of Mrs. Theodocopoulos who was our Sunday School teacher who tripped on the church pew during Easter Service. Well, I have no memory of that particular incident nor do I remember Mrs. T – but then we begin to talk about other people from our old community, and memories surface. A walk back to the past indeed.

Is it a coincidence as we reach this point in our lives, technology has made it so much easier to find people? It sure seems that way. Social media and the internet allow us to write a name in our search engine; a common name brings up many listings of the same name, so then you need to check each one out or make your search more defined.

I have done this numerous times with mixed results. Some are successful, some not. Some happy re-connections, some brought tears. Two people I was once close to in my childhood and in my twenties led me to their obituaries. Another childhood friend was tougher to find. Her Greek name was often coupled with an English version. The use of her real name was shortened. She changed her long, difficult-to-pronounce last name into her father's first name. I tried and tried to no avail. And then, one day, she found me! Happiness and Joy! She lives in another country, but we "chatted" and caught up with one another about our own lives and then moved into – are you in touch with other classmates? We shared what we knew, and then she told me that one of our dear school friends (my budding romance at the age of 12) was no longer with us – he had a hard life and an early passing. Tears flowed as I read her words.

Searching ancestry sites not only tells us about our family history, but it also connects us to a relative once or twice removed so we can connect with them as well and perhaps find out what happened to that branch of the family tree. Now that retirement brings more time to explore our past, the tools to do this are just right. Perfect Timing!

PS. 2020 Stay Home health emergency crises gives us the time to do this now!

SUNSET

Originally Published:

April 24, 2020

Being on social media more and more these days, I see what retired people and soon-to-be-retired people are worrying about.

Many of them are concerned with money – Will I/we have enough? How do I/we plan to have enough? I/we don't have enough, should I take Social Security now or wait? How do I keep my retirement safe? All very important questions. Responses to these posts vary – and although some of the advice sounds good, the best thing, in my opinion, is to speak to a professional. The cost might be a bit high, but if it keeps your money safe and helps you plan, it is well worth it. It will give you peace of mind.

Another issue that surfaces is what to do with all the "free" time they now face since they are not working… and even more so now, in this current environment of being safe at home. A few have said they don't want to travel or can't afford to. Others are isolated because work was everything to them, so they didn't have much family or friend interaction… and they are hesitant to reach out to them now. Some are bored and thinking about going back to work or finding some other kind of job but don't know how to get started with that. One person stated they can't get themselves motivated to search for things to do such as joining a book club, a bowling team, volunteering, or mentoring young people. And that brings us to another group of people.

Depressed, sad, lonely, and grieving. All very human and very real to say the least. And all very familiar to all of us in one way or another. I clearly remember certain periods in my life when I felt unable to function. Death of parents and other beloved relatives, work reverses, and romantic heartbreaks all played key roles in keeping me in a state of loss. That loss needed to be grieved and worked through which took time and effort.

Health is also mentioned – an issue that we all face daily. Some are just beginning this journey of aches and pains; some have been living with it for years, if not decades. It can indeed be debilitating, incapacitating, and hampering – our mind and our will want to take that walk, work in the garden, go shopping, go to the movies, etc. but our bodies prevent us from doing so. We keep all these people in mind and pray for their wellness.

Not everyone retires with a big fat checkbook or a spouse to share it with. Not everyone feels like going to the grocery store, much less to a Canasta card group. Not everyone has the health to live an active life. Those pictures we see in magazines, on TV, and online of couples dancing the night away on a cruise ship or resort veranda are not very realistic, as enticing as they may be. Not all of us can afford the trip, can't physically go on the trip, or don't want to go on the trip. We come in all sizes, shapes, and wallets.

Both Zaf and I are slowing down. We feel it every day… long days of work are especially tiring. We hit the couch early, right after dinner to relax. Not just the body but the mind – letting go of the day's issues, not thinking about tomorrow's issues, and simply just not talking about them to each other as we watch TV!

The key for me is to embrace this new slowness. To nurture myself as often as I can. To set boundaries as to what I can/will and what I can't/will do. We do have a full year ahead of us to get to retirement, so we are saving our energy for the big push later this year. In the meantime, we continue to explore what might be right for us – where we will live next, what travel plans would be financially feasible as well as physically realistic, what activities might be right for us, etc.

As the sun sets each day, we are grateful for what we have at hand. And we keep the faith that all will work out, as it often does in its way.

RE VS. RE

Originally Published:

May 8, 2020

I want to be retired but not retired. I don't want to revisit – I want to reinvent. I prefer to replace but not redo. It's better for me to reorganize but not to reprogram the regular old ways. I plan to replenish not rework.

I will not recapture my youth – I will redefine my future. I won't waste time trying to reverse my aging – I will revel in my years of experience. It's time for me to recollect my life and have no regrets.

Why go through the years ahead seeking to recover what once was and not recognize them as a time to rewire and redesign? I realize that it is easy to repeat and retrace remnants of a prior lifetime. To recall life's moments – good and bad – is a reminder of the way it was, but it is not a return trip.

I renounce and relinquish the recycling of useless reflections that, at best, reduce revelations of refreshing, relaxing, and rewarding adventures that rightly await us.

I reject the notion of restrictions acquired from living life to this point and relish a new sense of freedom.

I will keep treasured remembrances with respect as they are the roots of where I began – but the best way to give them the reverence that they deserve is for me to roll out more riches to living a well-rounded life, as an effort to redouble the importance of their humble lives.

The rehearsal is over; the curtain is rising towards renewal.

I am ruminating a completely new rebuild to the rhythm of my life – it's not a race to the finish, but a new route with resolute steps to reclaim the real me. I choose not to just rearrange the furniture, but to reupholster and reposition when we relocate to a new residence.

My goal is to review, reconsider, and reimagine my options, not regress into the same old routines. I am not reluctant to take the risk. The bell is ringing towards a new road to follow, a ramp rocketing up to rousing bouts of laughter, rocking and rolling with a new rhythm, traveling to riveting new vistas, and realizing that the world will soon see the rebranding of Helene.

I am open to receiving what the universe is willing to release. Roadways, airplanes, and rivers of the world will ferry us to the doors I choose to open. I am free to roam around the world.

I rejoice in the opportunity I have been graced with to grow old into a new reality. I will revive my body. I will resurrect my soul.

The Renaissance has begun.

HOW MUCH?

Originally Published:

June 12, 2020

We've been talking with our financial advisor about our retirement living finances and what needs to be done to be ready. So much to learn and comprehend. The biggest fear is not having enough to live on and even more important not having enough to see us through our lifetime.

I've always been a saver. As a single woman for over three decades, putting money aside was peace of mind. In the early years of building my business, I worked long hours. Two clients a day for business management services and at least 3 times a week. This was followed by seminar presentations, in the evenings, which I had to drive to throughout the Southern California region. Mom and Dad were good for a couple of meals a week, as were my sister and brother-in-law – eternally grateful to them. But, certainly, I was not going to rely on them for anything else; my parents were retirees and sis/bro were raising three children!

As I got older, I realized the saving pattern I had developed needed to be increased. But, how could I? House and car repairs loomed every time I turned around. Funds were needed to grow my business: website, marketing, production of a DVD and e-book, etc. The only way out was to get more clients – which increased the workload. It was an endless, vicious circle.

I plugged along. Eventually, new avenues opened where I could work smarter – less effort and more money! Then I got married. Zaf and I joined forces and created more sources of income for both of us. Savings increased, and things got better.

Here's what I learned from the financial expert:
Retirement Portfolio must be realistic. She had us create a retirement budget that was sensible, pragmatic, and prudent. First to do: How much money would be coming in and for how long. I'll still be working part-time so that is earned income, added to Social Security and IRA mandatory, and potential disbursement taken. The second up was to figure out what it would cost to sell the house/ buy a new house along with move-in costs which can be prohibitive. Mortgage/Utilities for our new home came next. Then the everyday living expenses were listed: food, clothes, cars, repairs and maintenance, household supplies, entertainment, travel, etc. The biggest section on this list was for medical insurance: medicare, secondary coverage, caretakers, long-term care, etc.

	PAYMENT, FEE WITHDRAWAL (–)	✓	FEE	DEPOSIT, CREDIT (+)	$ BALANCE
AP Automatic Payment					
BP Online Bill Pay					
T Online or Phone Transfer					
	$			$	$

The underlining point for all this preparation is the truth of the unknown: how long we will be around and what shape we will be in. We determined that our comfort level was to set everything up as though there was only one of us around to pay the bills. Exhausting and scary for sure. But we did it, and we now know what to expect. All things being equal, there are no major surprises.

Quite often, I see articles on social media, magazines, and newspapers on how to prepare for retirement. We Retire-Agers™ represent quite a large portion of the population so thankfully they provide invaluable information on the "best" way to retire… from finances to downsizing to staying active to exercising your body and brain to…… it's endless!

What is left now is to explore options and put the plan into action. Prep and sell house… pack the things we want to keep/get rid of the rest…decide where to move to… plan for our time living abroad… once again, it's endless!

THE YEAR BEFORE

Originally Published:

June 26, 2020

Back in September 2019, we decided that retirement would be happening in early 2021. In meeting that goal, there was much to consider and much to do. The more we talked, the more we convinced ourselves that we had plenty of time to explore, plan, decide, organize, and execute. We would give ourselves a year. And now, it seems like there is no time left at all.

In theory, everything sounded methodical, logical, and plausible. How finances would be handled, what to purge from the house vs. what to keep, our long-awaited dream of living abroad for a short while, where we would eventually move back to, how we would spend our time in retirement mode – it was discussed often and in earnest. Our RETIREMENT BOOK is brimming with ideas, contacts, and photos.

In reality, a lot has happened to throw us off our course. 2020 came in strong enough. I purchased bubble wrap, tape, and boxes to start the early packing – to get the items my nieces and nephew would be getting out of the house, ASAP! Then, a short while later, the world closed. The books to be donated to the library have been stacked in the garage for months, the bags of household items and clothes for a donation run to the nearest center lie along the stacks and next to furniture and assorted odds and ends. We can't get anything else in the garage, until what is in there is gone.

Places we wanted to visit, as potential moving sites, are not yet open for viewing. Virtual reality tours are nice enough and they all look so shiny and new; but until you see them in person, you simply don't know what you would be getting. A business we want to sell is not drawing any buyers yet. The business I want to keep is not growing because it depends on other businesses operating and thriving. Stymied, thwarted, and blocked…we are moving forward in slow motion.

The two things we did manage to do: remove the jacuzzi and repair the fence. All in the name of selling the home this fall, we have taken some steps to give it a face-lift. Each weekend we continue to clean out, clear out, and throw out. Zaf also wanted me to mention that he applied slurry to the driveway – twice! We have made calls to moving/storage companies to get a ballpark estimate on costs for moving our things out, keeping them in storage while we are away, and then moving them into our new home. I also have the name and phone number of a service that packs your house and coordinates with the moving company… wonder how much that costs!

Yesterday, I spoke to the pharmacy about getting enough medications for a lengthy stay abroad… an important issue!

Another big item on my to-do list is being totally mobile with my work needs. Getting everything online from books and manuals is not easy. Lots of copying, scanning, and saving. If I told you that I'm planning to save these materials in three different locations, would you think I'm neurotic? Probably. I just need to be sure that when we are on our journeys and I need to respond to a business question, my documents are completely accessible. Business? Yes, I'm only going to be semi-retired.

As of this writing, there seems to be a light at the end of the tunnel. With caution, things are opening up… each day brings keen anticipation of new opportunities, potential, and relief. Let's all keep a positive thought that all will go well.

In the meantime, I just ordered more bubble wrap!

September 2019

Sun	Mon
1	2
	Labor Day
	Labor Day
	Labor Day
	Labor Day
	Labor Day

BRAVO DADDY

Originally Published:

August 14, 2020

On November 25, 1997, I was given yet another reason to celebrate my Hellenic roots; the most compelling reason of them all. My father passed away peacefully, the very same way he lived his life. He was not a gregarious, bigger-than-life, Zorba-type Greek; rather, he was an old-world Greek who lived his life quietly, with inner strength, dignity, and much wisdom.

Last November, on a crisp winter day, I happen to be in Astoria, Queens – the famous Greek Town of New York City. In one of the many stores there, my eye caught sight of a small package of decals; they were heart-shaped with the American flag on one half of the heart and the Greek flag on the other half. Impulsively, I reached out, picked up a few, and put them in my shopping basket. That very evening, I got a telephone call that told me that my father had been admitted to the intensive care unit and that I should hurry home. A week later, I placed one of those decals on his final resting pillow, for he was the one who taught me how to love both countries.

With great care, we chose the plaque marking his grave; a Greek key adorns it. It is a message for all those who walk by to see – here lies an American whose spirit was Greek!   He was the inspiration behind the words I use every month in my column: My country is America; my heritage is Greece.

As a child, I received the gift of attending Greek Parochial School from 8:00am to 3:00pm daily. In second grade, I had to draw a map of Greece. I waited for him to come home from work and after a long 14-hour day, he rolled up his sleeves and drew a beautiful map of his homeland. He carefully printed the names of the big cities and as a tribute to his tiny village, he pinpointed a spot, high in the central mountains of Sterea Ellas, and wrote: MEGALO XORIO, KARPENISI. With a final flourish, he used a vivid blue crayon to color the beautiful Aegean Sea. Together, we beamed with pride. The map got an A+. He deserved it.

Once a year, on a hot summer Sunday, he would take a day off from work, and together, our little family of four would ride the subway to lower Manhattan. From there, we would take the ferry across the river and visit the Statue of Liberty. On a cold winter Sunday, we would wait in a long line to see the annual Christmas Pageant with the Rockettes at Radio City Music Hall, followed by a visit to the Rockefeller Center Ice Skating Rink. We would drink hot cocoa and make plans that someday, I too could skate there. And one day, a few years later, our dream came true. How easy he made it for me to be American and Greek at the same time!

By encouraging me to be both, I was set free from deciding to be one or the other. Thank you, Daddy.

He came to this country as an immigrant with a wife, two very young children, three suitcases, and thirty-five dollars in his wallet. He died a very rich man. Rich in faith, family, and friends.

Testimony to his faith was when the priests came to his hospital bed and began to pray. Dad, with his eyes closed, lifted his arm, which was attached to the various IVs, and made the sign of the cross. His family, surrounding him with love and respect, followed his direction once again and did the same.

At his birthday party a few years ago, 60 or so guests gathered around him as he blew out his 80 candles. Encouraged to make a speech, he raised his hand shyly and politely bowed his head. He did not thank anyone for their gifts or their good wishes. He simply said: "Thank you for bringing honor to our home." How can a child who hears these words and many others like them, not make family and home the cornerstone of her life? He will be in our hearts forever, as he was the heart of our home.

Evidence of his friends were the 49 cars in his procession from the church to the cemetery, the hundreds of flowers and baskets of food and bread, cards, letters and e-mails, donations to the Orthodox Church, the Catholic Church, a Jewish Synagogue, and the planting of trees. A very rich man indeed.

On the day he died, my mother hung his cross around my neck. It is a cross I gladly bear for many reasons. In life, he taught me to love America and to love Greece, for I was part of both. In death, he taught me how important the responsibility was to continue this message to the next generation.

A+ again. A job well done. Bravo daddy.

Helene K. Liatsos
Los Angeles, California

December 1997

My Country is America; My Heritage is Greece

In Loving Tribute To Her Father John Liatsos 1915 – 1997

"One generation passeth away, and another generation cometh."

– Ecclesiastes 1:4

MAY YOU HAVE MY BLESSING

Originally Published:

August 31, 2020

They say you become a woman the day your mother dies. I say that I became a woman when I stopped at a red light and looked in the rearview mirror. I saw my mother's face looking back at me. On that day, I finally knew who I was because I couldn't be who I was if she wasn't who she was.

Maria Priovolos was born in June 1917 in Micro Chorio, a small, picturesque village in the high mountains of Roumeli, a province located right in the heart of mainland Greece. A village so small, they gave it no other name than Micro Chorio – Small Village. The cobblestones and the well in the village square were her playground, but her childhood was short. Her father died when she was nine years old, leaving a young widow and three children, Maria being the eldest. She learned firsthand the hardship of life without a father, living on the hard work of her mother, and the generosity of relatives.

Although she often claimed to be an obedient and shy village girl, the stories she told us belied her very words. A true indicator of my mother's lively spirit and daring self is the story about the Fascists who had taken her pet lamb before setting up their headquarters in the church courtyard. Running down the hill and waving her arms, she entered the courtyard and stomped her feet, demanding that the little lamb be returned to her, immediately! The soldiers burst out laughing and one of the kinder ones took her by the elbow and led her back to her crying, anxious mother.

As a woman of marriageable age, she was sent to the Athenian relatives who could arrange for a husband. They cut off her braids and bobbed her hair. Maria was so horrified she spent the next year wearing a kerchief 24 hours a day. Alas, the men in Athens were much too hip to be attracted to a skinny village girl with the kerchief that never left her head. At the ripe old maid age of 29, an unwanted suitor presented her with a ring…the entire village rejoiced – this was, after all, possibly her last hope! But Maria threw the ring across the room, where it conveniently fell through the wooden floorboards. She wanted to marry for love…and so she did. My father, coming from the neighboring village for the annual village festival, took one look at my mother and they were married for 52 ½ years.

Alas, the men in Athens were much too hip to be attracted to a skinny village girl with the kerchief that never left her head. At the ripe old maid age of 29, an unwanted suitor presented her with a ring…the entire village rejoiced – this was, after all, possibly her last hope! But Maria threw the ring across the room, where it conveniently fell through the wooden floorboards. She wanted to marry for love…and so she did. My father, coming from the neighboring village for the annual village festival, took one look at my mother and they were married for 52 ½ years.

A relative arranged for their migration to America…dad went first. Maria followed John to America, for 18 days on a rocking ship with a toddler at her side and an infant in her arms. She lives in one small apartment after another in lower Manhattan… she walks 32 blocks in each direction to get to Central Park, so her children can play on grass.

John was the breadwinner and Maria was the heart-winner. She saved her money for the things that were important to her… sending her daughters to Greek Day School, so they could learn to read, write, and speak Greek. Each month, the daughters wrote letters to their two grandmothers, in Greek, under Maria's direction before she slipped a few dollars into the envelopes.

Fifty cents was spent each week on piano lessons for her daughters because she remembered the piano music she heard from the neighboring windows of a more well-to-do family in her hometown. And as one daughter played, she danced the waltz with the other. She fought, in Greek, to get her daughter into the Girl Scouts of America with a woman who obviously couldn't understand a word my mother was saying, but who did understand the meaning behind them; I became the first Girl Scout in our family.

She set aside time, each evening before we went to bed, to guide our little fingers into a three-point shape, so we could learn how to bless ourselves while we thanked God and each Sunday afternoon, after church services and lunch, she would turn on the radio to the weekly Greek program. As the music played, she taught her daughters how to do the Greek dances in the living room, 'round and 'round the coffee table. Holidays were the opportunities for her to train us on the intricacies of making the tiropita or the baklava. I remember her placing her hands over mine to demonstrate the best way to roll the dough into koulouriakia.

When my father came home dejected from a battle at the bank, my mother gave him an envelope with the $1000.00 she saved from the weekly allowance; together they bought our first house. When I was planning to go to my first dance, she ran around the corner to the five and dime in the pouring rain to get me a ribbon to match my dress. When I performed in plays and recitals, she came with flowers in hand, sitting in the front row, laughing and applauding when she saw others do it because she didn't understand a word. When my heart was broken, she slipped her hand into mine as we both watched a young couple with their arms around each other walking down the street. When my home was robbed, she stroked my hair and promised that she and Dad were with me and always will be.

When I was young and helpless, she fed, bathed, and changed me... when she was old and helpless, I did the same for her. She took my hand and led me to church, to school, and the dentist. I took her hand and led her to church, to the doctor, and to the cemetery to visit her husband. A mother's responsibility. A daughter's duty.

Maria Priovolos Liatsos died on February 3, 2003. There is so much that I remember; there is so much that I miss. But at the very top of that list is a simple phrase she would say was my indication that I had everything I needed to sustain me. It is what every child longs to hear even when we are grown adults. It is what she said when I first left home; it is what she said when I would take the time to visit with her so she could talk about the old days; it is what she said when I cleaned the accidents in the bathroom time and time again; it is what she said when I would tuck her in at night and we would nuzzle and giggle like little girls. The ache in my heart comes from knowing that for as long as I live, I will never, ever hear her say these words to me again: "May You Have My Blessing."

My Country is America; My Heritage is Greece

In Loving Tribute To Her Mother Maria Priovolos Liatsos 1917-2003

"One generation passeth away, and another generation cometh."   Ecclesiastes 1:4

SIMPLICITY

Originally Published:

September 18, 2020

With activity comes discovery. With discovery comes simplicity.

Our days are very hectic as we are planning to downsize into a smaller home. Our activity is going through closets, drawers, and the garage! First comes the sorting, and in doing so. I am making four piles. Pack for later usage, keep for usage now (then donate), donate/give away, and toss because it is of no use to anyone!

I discovered that we have six colanders, four manual graters, and four manual juice squeezers. So, I kept two colanders (one small and one large), one grater, and one juice squeezer. We do have an electric juice squeezer too – but just in case, we are keeping the manual one as well. The rest are to be given away. Picture me doing this with all the other items discovered in multiples! I can't even count the cutlery!!!

The dining room table has been converted to a tabletop display of all that is to be given away. Family members have been dropping by to pick out the things they want/need; sometimes I take a photo of them and they claim their items ahead of their visit. My one niece said it was like shopping online! What they don't take goes into the donation box.

My cousin Gus and his wife Joy sold their sprawling four-bedroom ranch home where they often saw deer playing in the back yard coming through the abutting wooded area; they moved into a two-bedroom townhome for 55+ and they love it! Gus told me that he discovered that they "only really use 2 rooms" and wonders why they didn't make the move earlier! No more yard maintenance, no more "packed to the rafters" garage, and no more empty nester bedrooms to dust for them…hurrah!

It is heartening to read and to speak with other Retire-Agers™ who have expressed the same opinion. Downsizing is the best thing they have done. To lead a simpler life is our due reward after a lifetime of collecting items we thought we absolutely must have or kept because a dear relative gave it to them and did not have the heart to throw it out. I too have lots of those, but thinking things through, I decided that it is not necessary to keep all the items to remember them and that others may need them more than I do.

As I began dinner the other night, I reached for a pot to boil some water and saw that I only had two of them – the ones I kept out for usage now. The joy that I experienced was profound! So easy, so effortless, so simple!

I already see how removing things from each of the rooms (getting ready to stage the house for potential buyers) makes them airier and fresher. I asked my five-year-old grand-nephew if he remembered coming to my house and he said yes he did. "It's old" were his exact words! I was thrilled he remembered it, but is that how I want to be remembered? Dark walls, lots of vintage furniture, etc. make for a classic style of décor – so me in lots of ways. But out of the mouths of babes comes a new discovery – make things lighter, brighter, and more simple!

"Pan Metron Ariston" – "In all things moderation," said an ancient Greek philosopher. And now, so many, many years after these words were first said, we are realizing what it truly means in all aspects of our lives. Without the clutter, we face fewer choices, less confusion, and less chaos, so we have the time to be active, to discover, and to simplify. Here's to exploring our retirement!

SIZE OF WALLET

Originally Published:

October 2, 2020

Our decision to move into a 55+ retirement community is firm. It promises to be an easier environment with noise, congestion, and more like-minded people. Retire-Agers™!!! We fear that a single-residence home could be in a neighborhood that suggests lots of children running around, cars dashing back and forth, and a house that needs more maintenance and repairs based on its age.

So, we visited a 55+ development this weekend. We've been watching it in development and as more and more information was released, we were able to see some floor plan options. Of course, I began to visualize furniture placement and some landscaping in the patio area!

Our choice, of course, is one level and smaller square footage than what we have now. What we saw was very nice, indeed; they showed you the updated version – all bright, shiny, and new. The plans that I thought I liked on paper and a virtual tour were not our first choice when we saw them in person; the one plan that I didn't like turned out to be the best one! Go figure!

The rooms were smaller than we imagined. We found ourselves measuring the floor space, placing one foot in front of another because we forgot to bring a measuring tape. What my eyes saw was how we would arrange the furniture and soon realized that most furniture that we own must be left behind. When we say downsize, we mean downsize!

This was hard to take at first, I spent the night thinking about what I should let go of and how I felt about it. I woke with a more determined approach to finding new homes for our things.

The cost of these homes is not cheap… and doesn't save you any money. They cost about the same as a single-residence home in a nice neighborhood. The models reflect the upgraded version, but they quote you the base price. On average, the rep told us, the upgrades can go up to another 60K… What? That was an Ouchy! Do we really need the optional French doors or the super-duper shower faucet? Hmmmmm…. Everything is brand new, so you won't have the potential maintenance and repair of an older home… but still, that is a lot of money.

Then we have the HOA dues. You must evaluate what you get for another monthly payment. Will you use the clubhouse and all the facilities there? Will you join in on all the activities? What else does it cover? Some landscaping, some basic utility – and that's about it.

I calculated what we pay now for gardener, pest control, etc. and it comes out to be a little less than their fee, but then again, we don't have a gated entrance or common areas to pay for.

I was thinking that a downsize of a home and lifestyle would leave more funds in our wallet for travel, activities, and fun! We have educated ourselves to the fact that this might not be the case. One should never be "house poor" but that is what this seems like. It emphasizes the importance of retirement exploring to make sure that all the pieces fit into this new journey.

A shift in our thinking is taking place. It's time to completely let go of the old and bring in the new, into a smaller home so we can be truly successful in downsizing in every way to accommodate our physical stamina, state of mind, and our wallet so we can retire well.

YOU CAN DANCE TO IT!

Originally Published:

October 30, 2020

A social media group friend asked me how I felt about parting with my home, my household goods, and my life as I have lived in this house. My reply was that on some days I am highly motivated to clean it all out – to sort what I am keeping from what is to be donated or thrown out, to stage the house for selling, and along the way find all the treasures I have amassed over the years. On other days, while going through the same routine, I am overwhelmed with melancholy as I am flooded with memories and recollections of the past. This, alas, is part of retirement.

One day, I decided to play some music as I began the never-ending list of things to do. I started with my favorite – Dean Martin – who always brings on a smile. My first celebrity crush since I was eleven years old, a continuous fantasy of someday meeting him in person (I never did – but I did see him several times at various restaurants – be still my heart!) and indeed, the one song that he is most famous for where everybody loves somebody sometime was our first wedding dance! On these days, I accomplish a lot as I sing along and feel the beat.

Classical music brings on another mood. Calming, purposeful, and an immense feeling of peace. That these melodies are ageless and that I will survive, as they have.

Greek music has been in my life since birth. It lifts my feet and connects me to generations of family members who danced the way I learned to dance. From my earliest recollections, I remember how on Sunday afternoons, after church and lunch, my mother would turn on the radio and listen to the Greek program. When they played music, she would take my sister and me by the hand and lead us in Greek dancing around and around the coffee table. We dance in circles – it always brings us back to where we started from and represents the continuation of life… and so, a lifelong love it remains to this day.

What is most colorful is music from other countries. Romantic Italian and French love songs speak to me even though I don't understand much. Cha-cha's, rumbas, salsas, etc. bring a bigger picture of how the world is much smaller when we love each culture and enjoy what it has to offer.

Music from the 70s to the present had some really good sounds, but then again some awful stuff… with all the screeching and hollering. You had no idea what they were saying and what all the fuss was about. Listening to some of the best of those years is fun, but inevitably we go back to our own growing-up years.

What can I say about rock and roll? My life, my era, my past. Each song brings on a memory of the specific time and place of when I first heard it. Having an older sister, all these 45s were in the house in plentiful. The Jitterbug, the Lindy, the Stroll, the Twist, the Watusi, the Frug, the Mashed Potato – we had them all and they were endless because we still have those 45s and plan to use them for fellow Retire-Agers™ at the oldies nights we plan to host.

Nothing compares to that rock and roll beat. It's classic and represents an era in American history that changed music forever. A memory of holding on to a doorknob as I danced to the beat of my favorite record remains firm in my mind – what else could I do when I couldn't find a partner!? The other night, the TV blared the unforgettable rhythm of an oldie; I jumped up off the couch and danced around the living room. I pointed out to Zaf, that I – a Retire-Ager™ – can still rock and roll with the best of them. He smiled and said yes, I can see that you still got it!

I read somewhere that music is a healer. It is played when people are ill, troubled, and hurting. It reaches the very core of us and lightens up the heart. My nephews and nieces were held with much love when they were young, but what they remember the most is when I sang to them. Their sweet little eyes would shine brighter, and giggles would follow. Silly me, who sang and danced them around the room, created a memory they will remember forever.

The universal language of music crosses all barriers, not only real ones that divide people and countries but the soul and heart of people everywhere. That is why no matter what music I listen to, I dance to it.

THE WHOLE OF ME

Originally Published:

November 13, 2020

Zaf came home and asked me what I was doing. Sitting at my desk, after spending the entire morning cleaning out the "office area" of the garage and dragging the boxes into the office, I was tearing through paperwork stored for over twenty years.

My hands were busy going through each file, separating papers that had personal information on them and stacking them in, yet another pile headed for the shredder.

But my mind was visiting my former life.

Tax returns, mortgage payments, income earned, utility bills, office expenses, etc. re-visited my/our financial history. I can certainly understand keeping recent tax records, but why on earth was I keeping a receipt for a coat I bought a decade ago? It was interesting to see mortgage rates from 2000 and what it cost me to refinance in 2008, but it is time to toss them out and focus on upcoming financial retirement plans.

Old addresses brought flashes of rooms that I lived in, cleaned, hosted family and friends, and sought comfort in after long, busy days making a living and living life.

Paystubs from jobs that I took on the side to support myself as I established my business were reminders of how hard I worked to change the way I earned my living... from being an employee to being able to support myself as a business owner was a long road. Seeing the awards of achievements given to me made me proud – yet humbling; they motivated me to help others start and grow their own business and give them the tools to succeed.

Old clients greeted me and reminded me of the time I spent with them, how much they paid me, and wondering where they are today. Are they still in business? Have they retired? Did they move away? Should I get a minute in my hectic days, I might just use social media to find them.

The items I kept were my day runners. Yes, they may not call them that now, because not too many people use them – everything is on mobile phones. It is indeed easier to use as you carry your phone anyway, except for the tiny keyboards that tend to pop in a word you didn't intend to use – so you have to keep typing to get to the word you do want to use! I don't carry the day runner with me either… I keep it on the side credenza near my desk and record key points of my days as I have done since the beginning of time. The past entries I have made bring me back to how I lived each day… a walk down memory lane… and one that I will use to find inspiration for my blog. I like my blog to be based on how we explore retirement days ahead by reflecting on where we were yesterday. The rhythm of the two intertwines the past, the present, and the future. It is the whole of me.

The piles got smaller and smaller and finally disappeared. But I am still here, embracing a new way of living, and finding freedom from carrying the weight of the past from things that don't really matter. Exploring what comes next is highly anticipated!

I didn't hurry though. I looked at each page and enjoyed the memory jolts. You would think that all this delving into the past would bring tears to my eyes. No, the tears I shed were because the shredder was heating up too fast, getting caught in its own cycle and driving me nuts. Retire well.

RETIRE-AGERS™ ROUTINE

Originally Published:

December 4, 2020

We are bombarded daily with reminders to exercise daily. Getting into a routine takes much effort and time – something I don't have much to spare right now. But I've come up with something else – it's what I call the Downsizing Movement Program.

I started with the office closet. Standing on my little red step stool, I STRETCHED by REACHING the top shelves. In addition, I did some serious TWISTING of the entire body to get to the corners. This was followed by extreme arm and body motion when LIFTING and HAULING down the crates filled with paper, folders, etc. HEAVING them onto the desk was another movement that left me breathless.

To clean out the lower section, I did a whole series of BENDING and SQUATTING; these were done several times to finish the job for the day. They say all exercises should be done as repetitions, so I was on it! These items had to be hauled to the desk as well, so that must account for something.

Also, let's not forget all the STEPPING I did on and off the step stool – there must be some points for that!

This entire routine repeated throughout the house over the next few days. The second bedroom was attacked, but it wasn't as bad as the office. The master bedroom was a real chore; I had to separate clothes into piles after they were removed from the closet, the shelves, and the drawers. Because we are selling the house and planning a major trip next year, I had to determine which clothes to be stored and which ones were being kept aside for the trip (not to mention what we need to wear now)… all of this was determined by the seasons – fall, winter, spring and summer – and where we would be at any given point. A lot of TOSSING ensued.

Extra credit was given when I slipped off the step stool and fell into the remaining hanging clothes that broke my fall, and left me with a big gash on my arm. This was a RAPID ARM movement exercise which necessitated a short break and a cool adult beverage to rehydrate my body, which is highly touted by health and nutrition gurus everywhere.

Once the items in all the rooms were identified, they had to be boxed up and DRAGGED to the garage… I say dragged because CARRYING them was not an option. Once in the garage, I decided to leave them on the floor, so my husband can get some exercise when he LIFTS them to the shelves and/or the back of the car when he takes some of them to the donation centers.

When I began the journey of exploring retirement, this routine was not on the top of the list of things to do… it was more fun and exciting to plan our trip, visit potential new homes, dream about new activities to discover, and, of course, blog. Alas, I soon discovered that to get to that point, I had to work towards it. So here I am, knee-deep in bubble wrap and boxes, sorting out our life by using the Downsizing Movement Program.

The good news is that this effort was accomplished; the bad news is now I need to find another routine to replace it. I suspect I will as the garage is filled to the rafters.

I am a strong believer in the reward system for a job well done. Since I am self-employed, I get to choose the reward. I choose to Retire Well!

BYE BYE

Originally Published:

January 19, 2021

Last view of our home as we drive away. Sold, packed, and moved in 45 days. A milestone achieved with much anxiety (will we close escrow on time?) and exhaustion (I can't believe how much we still had to pack, throw out, donate, etc. It was endless!) But we did it and are off to the next step of our retirement adventure.

There were just a few moments that got to me. As the movers took out the last piece of furniture from the bedroom, I sat on the large window sill and looked into the bathroom area which I designed and loved. Black and white tiles on the floor. The Greek Key design borders around the tub and shower. A beautiful mirror with ancient Greek columns. I flipped back to the time when I poured over design tiles to pick just the right one and worked with the contractor to get it all just right. My eyes welled up.

When our next-door neighbor of twenty years came over, wearing her mask and holding a bottle of wine, I burst into tears; she did as well. Her good-luck card was filled with sweet messages promising a continued friendship no matter where we lived.

And then, when the moving trucks left and Zaf and I stood in the driveway prepared to drive away, I broke down. Sobbing on his chest, I mourned and grieved the past as the past, and finally pulled away with a smile and faced the future.

We're in temporary housing for a few months, settled in and making ourselves comfortable. A new rhythm to our lives already feels lighter as we now begin to plan for our trip in March: dates, places, transportation, people to contact, vaccinations, international driving licenses, etc. Two years ago, we contemplated living abroad for six months – we hashed out the pros and cons time and time again. And then, one night, after a long day of work, we made the monumental decision to make it happen. What are we waiting for? – we asked ourselves. And so we began to explore.

When and how do we tell our clients that we are going to stop working? When do we put the house up for sale? When do we go to Greece? Where do we live between the sale of the house and our departure date (Where we are now)? Decisions, decisions, decisions!

Taking one step at a time, and facing some delays, we have made progress. There were so many days (and nights!) I thought "this will never happen," but the same focus and perseverance both Zaf and I have had in our lives to accomplish many things was applied and here we are!

Unbelievable! And yet, we aim to Retire Well.

WEIRD

Originally Published:

February 8, 2021

We are living in temporary housing surrounded by suitcases and boxes. It feels very strange being in someone else's house. When I said we would be exploring in our retirement, this was not exactly what I had in mind – but still, it was fun opening cabinets and closets to find treasures.

We have chosen a space where you could realistically live full time – it's really very nice with a good sized living room and adjoining dining area, a full kitchen and all the appliances you need. It has a washer and a dryer, a large bedroom, walk-in closet, and a good size bathroom.

Our hosts have provided every amenity: coffee, creamer, sugar, salt and pepper, cooking oils, tin foil and plastic wrap, garbage bags, paper towels, etc. All the dishes, cutlery, glasses cups, etc. are brand new. In the bathroom, there is a full supply of soaps, shampoos, conditioners, toilet paper, etc. The linens are all fresh and clean. It has a lovely patio to sit in with lots of plants and greenery all around. It's all very comfortable and inviting.

But still – it's not home… which is rather peculiar since we don't have a home right now! We sold our home last month, stored our favorite things, packed our bags, and here we are. It took about a day or so to acclimate to a smaller space with a different routine. We do very little cooking – mostly take-out. We buy smaller amounts of food and other items for our daily use.

What is even more startling is when my laptop flashes pictures of our former home. I've taken pictures of all the rooms over the years as we redecorated and during family gatherings. The dining room where all the bookcases aligned the windows and the two tables that were joined together to create one long holiday table is my favorite because it reflects the happy family faces as they enjoyed my home-cooking and gave thanks.

I told myself and then Zaf... get used to it!

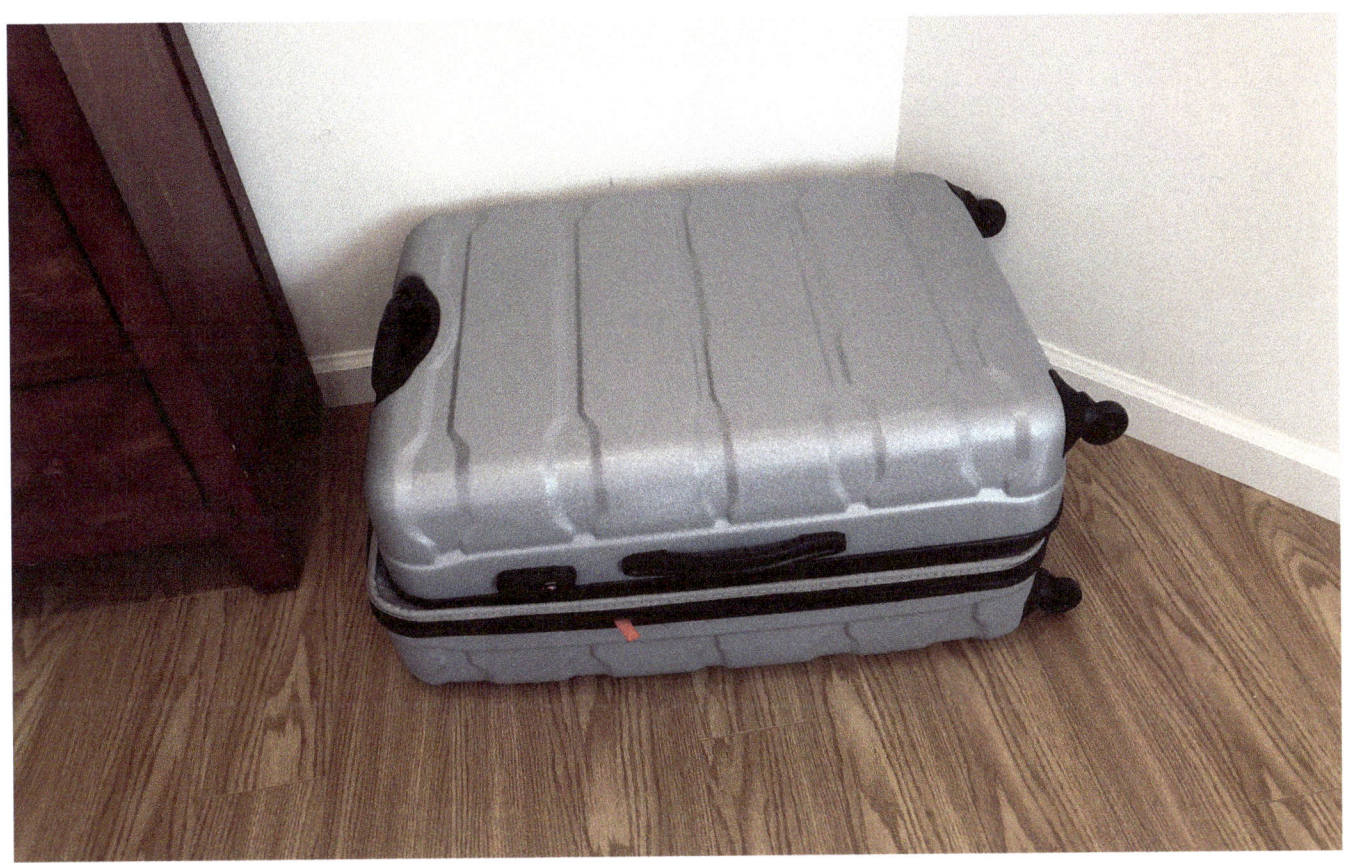

We are vagabonds for the next 8 months… going to Greece and Southern Europe, it will be hotels all the way. Most offer breakfast with the price of the room which is nice to enjoy as you sit on the balcony or patio and look at the view of the blue sea or the majestic mountains. The perfect setting to pour over brochures to see what we should explore that day.

It does tug at my heart on some days when I see those photos – nonetheless, the die is cast. We are on the first leg of our retirement journey. What we planned over the last two years is finally here. Yikes! And Yeah!

WINDING DOWN AND UP

Originally Published:

March 1, 2021

You might ask how both things can be happening at the same time, but it is true. We are winding down our old way of living and are winding up to our new adventure – exploring retirement!

Indeed, we have spent the better part of the last two months winding down – from selling the house, closing all the accounts (utilities, services, etc.), packing up items for storage, discarding/donating items we no longer can use, packing clothes and essentials for the almost three-month stay in temporary housing and then pre-packing our clothes and essentials for our six-month trip. Exhausting? To say the least.

Even so, there are several items still waiting to be finalized. We planned on selling our cars right before we left. But life sends a curve ball now and then. Zaf was in an accident – he is just fine, but the car (mine!) was totaled. That was not part of the original plan, so we had to regroup after the initial shock.

Because the car was so old, we did not have collision coverage; I scrambled around looking for a junk car dealer and finally found one that offered a decent price. Now, I've got to go to the motor vehicle department and deal with all of that! When Zaf sells his car, we then need to cancel the auto insurance.

Moreover, making sure that all entities we are part of, such as social security and supplemental medical insurance, have our new address (we are using my sister's address for now) is a daunting task. It's a long, long list and every day I remember yet another company I have to call. This winding down seems to go on and on and on!

Hence, if you are like me, you don't realize the number of places where you are listed and how much of your information is out there in the universe. This is a good time to delete, cancel, consolidate, etc.

Business Beckons Too!

One of our businesses is being taken over by some lovely people who will be managing it for us – we are very lucky to have found them! Blessed for sure, but there is work to be done. I've got to lay out the whole system for them: daily activity recap, train them on payroll, pre-pay some bills, contact the vendors to assure them they will all get paid, and make sure the employees are happy!

At the same time, I've got my own work to do. My trainings and consultations continue. Remember, my retirement is part-time, and the icing on the cake is that everything is done online, so I never have to leave home! I check in every morning, take care of business, and then am free for the rest of the day. This new change of pace and less stress has given me a greater sense of peace and contentment.

I could also throw in the "work" that I do for my blog – but is it really? Nah, just a great way to chronicle our retirement journey and share it with you! I enjoy writing; it's fun trying to figure out a photo that will work with what I am saying, and I love sharing it all with you – so no, it's definitely not work!

Trip Prep

The winding-up part is getting ready for the trip. Double-checking passports (I did this three times!) came first. Reviewing our flights online and making a paper copy.

Tucking into my suitcase a copy of the family tree – what I have so far – to update and revise with my Greek relatives and make sure that all their names and phone numbers are in my Big Brown Notebook.

I started this book two years ago when we made the monumental decision to sell everything and spend six months in Greece, as a springboard to our retirement life. In it, I've listed all the places where we have been before and more importantly, all the places we want to see for the first time. Meteora is a prime example… look it up and see for yourself how amazing it is!

Speaking of the "notebook." Italy is a part of it. As I read about a hotel or a restaurant or a site to see in a magazine or on social media, I would make a note of it and all those notes were put into a large white box. Well now, I've transferred them into their own little section and they serve as a little peek into what awaits us on our travels to Tuscany and its environs.

It's good to reassure myself that I have also recorded the contact info for family and friends who will be getting postcards from wherever we are, so they can follow along on our itinerary.

Other items we had to investigate and set into place were a few hotel stays, renting a car, getting international driver's licenses, exchange rate, and use of ATMs… all good now but harrowing when they loomed up at me from my many lists of things to do!

Additionally, looking into travel medical insurance has been an eye-opener… it's Not Cheap! Eventually, I found something decent and purchased it… a necessity for sure. We have packed a smaller suitcase with all our medical supplies – mostly needed pills and vitamins, but band-aids, pain relievers, etc. are in there too. I keep adding as Zaf says: "They have band-aids in Italy now."

Future Home

Another wind-up activity: we bought into a 55+ development for our future home. We are kept busy deciding what cabinets, flooring, countertops, etc. we want. It is amazing what choices are available, at different price points for sure, but still, I felt like I was on an episode of a home decorating TV show.

The location is about a half hour away from where we are now, so we try to go in the afternoons. We then spend some time driving around our new neighborhood getting familiar with where the supermarkets and banks are; I found the library and Zaf found several golf courses!

Going over our selections is nerve-racking. Did we make the right decisions? Will the alabaster white color go with the grey backsplash? Is the quality of the flooring worth the cost? Hours of sleep were lost as I tossed and turned, but mornings bring confidence as I look at the materials at hand and am happy with our choices.

Meanwhile...

The undercurrent to all of this is the pandemic, of course. When we started two years ago, in thinking through the steps we had to take to get to this point, we did not anticipate this concern. And yet, we are moving forward. We have taken both vaccine doses, wear masks and sometimes gloves, stay away from people as much as we can, and pray for the best. We also check to see what travel restrictions we can expect; we will be doing our testing before we take off and hope for the best. We do have EU passports so that might help, but you just never know. We'll see – I'll let you know how the entire thing plays out.

Let's all live out loud and Retire Well.

ETD

Originally Published:

March 19, 2021

Our departure was on time. Here is Zaf unloading the suitcases at the airport. Our retirement adventure begins! The first thing we explored was the way check-in was handled… and I am happy to report it was very well-organized with staff directing our way through the maze. Travel is always a hassle, but so far so good.

Safe Space

Not only were we guided through the process, there were very few people; we all followed the six-feet rule. Everyone I saw was wearing a mask. One jerk tried to get ahead of someone else and he was asked to leave; he became belligerent but enough staff/security got around him so he turned around and left, spewing bad words over his shoulder. Honestly, some people are just too self-absorbed… for them, it's all about me, me, me!

Roomy

Typically, when we book seats, Zaf and I always select aisle and window – playing the odds that no one picks the middle seat. Sometimes nobody does, so it is empty, but sometimes someone does, and then we ask if they can switch and give them the option of a window or aisle so we can sit together. This time though, the middle seat was already empty because the airline wouldn't allow it to be selected so it was great! We did not have to play armrest shuffle!

We ate the same thing.

They gave us a snack – an energy bar, some nuts, and a bottle of water. 3.5 hours later, they gave us the very same snack! No variance, no choices, and no extras. Oh well, it cut off the hunger pangs for the time being… better than nothing.

Are We There Yet?

We did not have to ask this question. We left on time and got to Boston in record time: 4 hours and 53 minutes! Under five hours coast to coast! I guess there was no traffic!

Not Sure Why…

We got our double doses of the vaccine; we tested negative as well. It seems a bit nonsensical though… we take a test 72 hours before the flight. We then go about our business and could be exposed to the virus. We get our results back as negative because at that moment in time, it was. Nobody asked us about the results of our test before boarding and nobody asked us when we deplaned five hours later; they just made an announcement saying that we need to self-quarantine if we are positive and they trust us to do the right thing. Well, we did – we got the shots and the negative test, so I put all our paperwork back in my bag. We put our masks on and left the airport.

Kick-off!

And so, we began our retirement journey. We are now visiting family and friends as we once again explore New England. Our aim is to retire well.

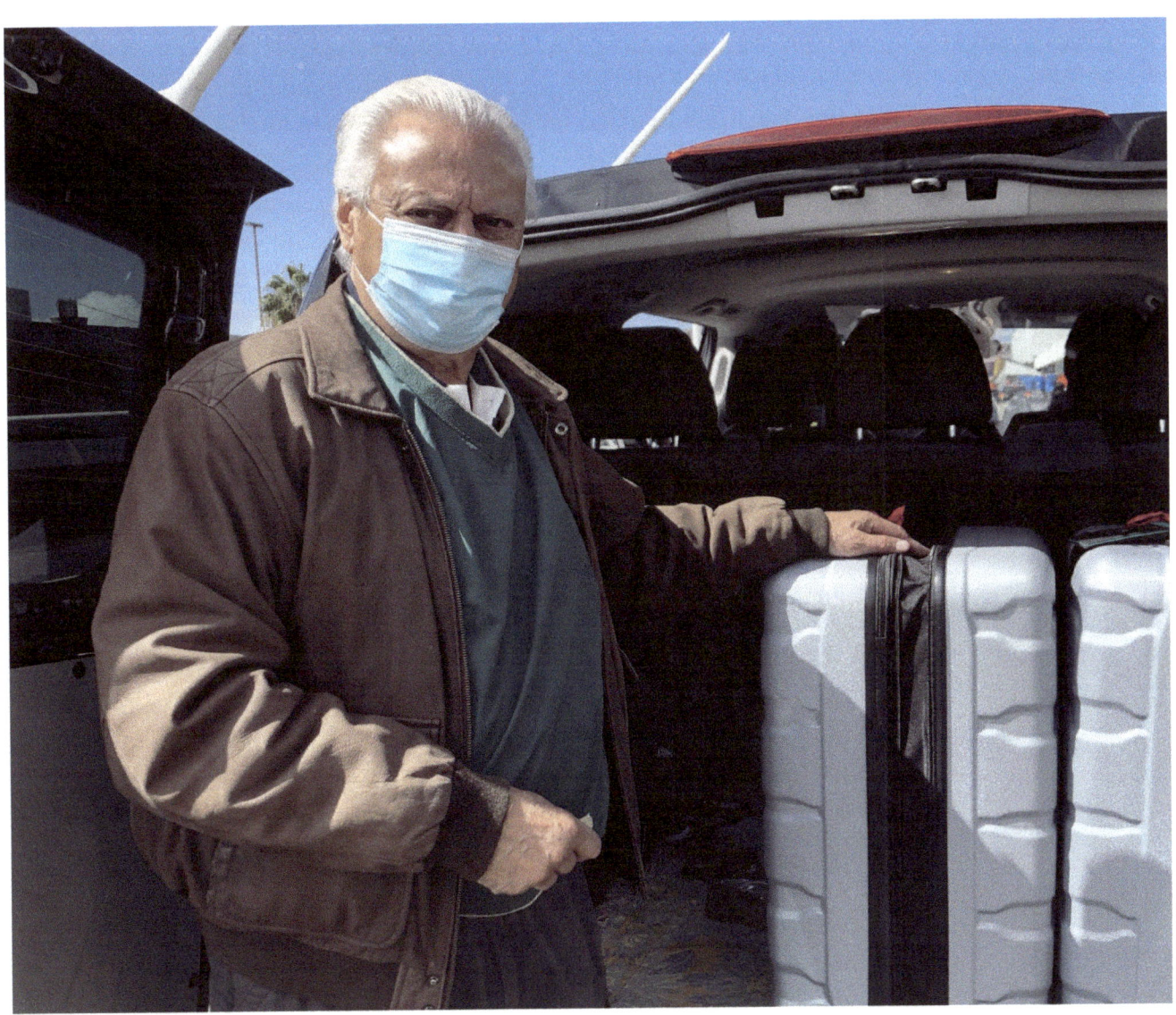

WE TOUCHED HISTORY

Originally Published:

March 27, 2021

Our dream of being in Greece on March 25th, 2021 came true as we celebrated the 200th anniversary of Greece's independence from the Ottoman Empire. While not being able to be at the very spot of the parade and presentations due to COVID restrictions, we were allowed to visit later in the day so we could touch history.

Everyone Knows

Television and social media have shown us how this day is being celebrated throughout the world – the blue and white lights of Greece have lit up the skies! The key speakers from representatives of various countries – Britain, France, etc. – all spoke of how bravely the Greeks fought when the spark of the revolution took hold from a small town that spread rapidly throughout the country. How determined they were to rid themselves of the hold of occupation by a foreign army; how men, women, and children stood up to an enemy in their midst for over 400 years.

It was time to take back their country, and history was made with every battle won until Greece was free.

Pride

We stood amongst the flags as the national anthem was played and felt a tug in our hearts that echoed back to our ancestors with whom we share DNA. Everything we went through from all the craziness of sorting and packing, selling our home and cars, divesting ourselves of business interests, paring down our possessions, etc. was worth this very moment in our own history of being here on Greek soil, on the day of Independence 2021.

All of Hellas

We are free to roam around the country – Greece = Hellas – because our forefathers and mothers rose up and took back their land as they called out "Freedom or Death."

Athens is filled with history everywhere we go, and we relish every corner we turn. In just a few days of being here, we have re-familiarized ourselves with the streets, the squares, and the sites we have seen before. It says a lot when we know which street to take to get to any destination. It is perhaps innate.

The people here are warm and hospitable. They greet us everywhere we go, and once they find out that we are ethnically Greek, the cheers go up; we start rapid speaking in Greek to each other! We are at home 6000 miles away from home.

In a few days, we are off to Thessaloniki, the second biggest city in Greece - where Zaf's family comes from. It is about a five-hour drive due north. About halfway up, we drive past Lamia where I was born. We don't stop there this time as we plan to return to that area and go higher into the mountains where the villages of my parents are located deep in the wooded areas in all their splendor.

The call for freedom is the core of retirement. Our days are our own; we do, we go, we sit, we nap, we cook, we eat, we bike, we dance, we play cars, we golf, we whatever! Zaf and I feel blessed as our plans fell into place, and we are now at the start of our retirement exploration. We enjoy sharing it with you and hope to hear from you as well.

ZAF'S HOMETOWN

Originally Published:

April 5, 2021

A five-hour drive from Athens to the north brought us to Zaf's hometown just outside the city of Thessaloniki. We purposefully set out on a Sunday morning when traffic is typically minimal, and coupled with the lock-down of citizens who are not permitted to go from one state to another, the road was practically empty. Two pit stops along the way, we arrived in the late afternoon and then spent half an hour looking for our hotel.

Kerasia

Zaf's birth village is called Nea Mehaniona; he grew up in Kerasia one town over. The area has changed with new buildings and other structures, and with old landmarks shuttered down, we drove around a little bit. Bad directions from a woman who insisted that the hotel was through some narrow roads and then off to the right by the beach led us to become a bit lost. A kind man called the hotel for us and got the correct directions; absolutely beautiful, but nowhere near the beach!

Memories

The next day, we toured all the villages in the area and found Zaf's memories… some places still exist, and others have disappeared forever. Wherever you go in these areas, you have a view of the magnificent Thermaic Gulf AKA Gulf of Salonika. Peaking through the clouds early in the morning when they float away, the entire city comes into view with its full impact of how big it is and how lovely it sits with its white buildings and blue sea as a neighbor. More about this beautiful city later as we return to it several times during our stay in Greece.

Mr. L

The highlight of our stay here was finding Zaf's lifelong friend, Mr. L. His wife and he greeted us with much exclaim and many hugs (yes, indeed!). We sat on their veranda as they reminisced about their childhood together as boys of eight and nine. They played soccer together on a dirt road that today is the main street running through the village. We discovered that we can now talk more often, once we are back in the USA, through social media channels as Mr. L. has now joined the 21st century.

Desserts

We are living in a lock-down environment; the bustling restaurants and tavernas we experienced before are closed. Our slow entry into this beautiful country has led us to places where we order takeaway or get delivery to our hotel room. Included in the menu options are the most amazing Greek desserts… naturally, we had to try some. For all the restrictions, life can be delicious!

Exploring retirement should include all types of experiences; the food here is absolutely amazing. I will share more about Greek desserts – with photos – as we travel about.

KASTORIA

Originally Published:

April 11, 2021

A beautiful city on the lake in northwestern Greece in the region of Western Macedonia…about a two-hour drive from Salonika with a pit stop in Edessa (another visit there later on this year will be on my blog for it). A truly lovely sight where the entire city is built around a very large lake; shops and restaurants rim the strand where long walks beckon as you watch the geese go by. Kastoria is a place we visit every time we come to Greece.

Antiquity

Written mention of this city/area dates back to the 11th century, but it could very well have been there long before it was ever mentioned in history books. Numerous Byzantine churches abound in this area. One particular one, which we visited on a prior trip, is built into the mountain with an amazing small door that almost cannot be seen with the naked eye. Tiny but most holy as the mosaics there have been in excellent condition for the ten centuries of its existence.

Where We Stay

Snow comes to this part every winter and the lake freezes over. A late spring blooms and the place comes alive with tourists and citizens flooding the entire city where numerous hotels can be found at very reasonable prices. Some newly built hotels are available and although Zaf prefers these, I like the older, more charming ones – often the B and B's, guest houses, or my personal favorites - the mansions dating back to the 18th century that are now the boutique Hotels of Greece.

Our hotel is over 200 years old; a former home of some very important and wealthy family at the time, it was purchased by an enterprising young man who turned it into a boutique hotel with many original pieces in place and an abundance of updates for modern conveniences. As with other hotels we have stayed at so far, we were reminded of the lockdown restrictions in place – but when not "looking" allow us some trespasses…nothing major, just some minor adjustments!

Shopping or Not!

Kastoria is known for the fur industry and although this is not very popular in many places around the world, it is indeed a flourishing industry. Warm slippers are a must-buy for Zaf and they last a really long time. I tried on a really beautiful vest but alas, it did not fit and there was nothing larger…bummer!

We spent a pleasant day here walking around and browsing the windows of some of the closed shops, ate some delectable food, had a good night's rest, and off we went to our next stop two hours southwest of Ioannina.

EPIRUS

Originally Published:

April 26, 2021

Spending five days in the prefecture called Epirus was a balance between total relaxation and scaring me senseless! This area of Greece is on the western side of Northern Greece between the Pindos Mountains and the Ionian Sea. We drove here from Kastoria, which took about an hour and a half of rainy weather and some interesting landscape along the way among dotted small villages and farmland.

Ioannina

Ioannina is the capital of Epirus, and that was our destination. It is a big city filled with hotels, museums, restaurants, cafes, and a lot of shops. It has two key features: the lake and the castle, known as Kastro in Greek.

Lake Pamvotis has a long shoreline with a walking path, a cycling path, and one-way traffic which helps a lot when you are going in that direction; if not, you have to go all the way around the Kastro!

On the lake is an island where Ali Pasha built his home inside a fortress complete with canon holes and other bits of armory. He was the Ottoman ruler from 1740 until Greece's revolution for Independence in 1821. A ferry boat takes you there, and you can visit the house (restored) and the museum with artifacts, costumes, jewelry, and documents of that period. There is also a tiny sweet chapel where you can rest and find a little peace knowing what a difficult time it was for the Greek people living there.

The Kastro is the citadel built in 528AD by Ali Pasha as his headquarters and command post. Today, it is a must-see place as you go through the enormous gates and wander around the winding cobblestone streets to see the lovely, charming homes; churches and a synagogue can be visited as well as a museum with relics collected dating back centuries.

Itinerary

After we checked into our charming "mansion" hotel, we relaxed with a walk down to the lake. I say "mansion" because that is what they call homes built over 200 years ago and now restored as luxury

hotels with much of the remaining original household items of the people who owned the homes over the years on display.

We planned our itinerary around the weather. A bit drizzly one day so we leisurely walked to the shopping area and browsed; most stores were closed due to the lockdown, but we enjoyed just being there and stopping for delicious ice cream!

The next day, it was rainy again, but we decided to head out into the glorious Pindos Mountains. I've always wanted to visit a town called Metsovo, on the eastern range, so that is where I went. Absolutely freezing cold! We had seen snow up on the mountain tops, of course, but this town is so way up there. There was snow on the ground, on the cars and trees, and the rooftops. Tiny, twisting roads took us so far; I jumped out, took some pictures, and jumped back in the car! I was disappointed that we could not get further into the town as it is built on the side of the mountains with homes strewn from one end to the other and on top of each other. When you see it from afar, it is absolutely beautiful.

I thought the climb up that mountain was scary enough – but I was wrong! The next day was even worse!

Pindos

Pindos Mountain is a series of rugged mountains ranging from 3000 to 7000 feet. This entire region is called Zagori (Zahgoree – with the accent on the ee). It has about 40 villages scattered throughout the highly forested mountains that live among the natural beauty of this area. All the villages together are known as Zagorochoria. None of them are flat; they are built into the mountains at different levels so they are on top of each other with tiny roads intertwining them.

Zaf and I had seen a movie filmed in this area, and we fell in love with the natural streams, crystal-clear rivers, bridges, rocky gorges, and breathtaking views. What you think is fog is a light mist that emanates throughout the mountains as the endless twists and turns take you up and up and up. You feel that you are on top of the world.

That is when I had my eyes open and not clutching the door handle – the drop-down was absolutely frightening, and you can only wonder: how do people from this area go up and down these roads to get to the city? Do they go once a week? A month? Holidays? Once a year? But then again, they wake up to magnificent sunsets and get to see the glorious sunsets behind the mountains every day!

Take the Shot

Taking pictures here was a challenge. The views were incredible, but where do you stop to enjoy them? Certainly not on the curves! We had to find a small inlay on the road so we could pull over, maneuver the car into place, and take the shot. Zaf would often encourage me to take photos while he was driving as we passed so many places where we felt we were in a dream. I would look at him aghast! He was on the inside of the road while I had a bird's eye view of the drop-down into the frightening gorges and canyons below. My hands were in a knot as was my stomach… the camera was just lying on my lap; there was no way I was going to make any moves.

Weren't We Just Here?

Getting lost was easy to do; so many turns, not enough signage, and keeping an eye on the road leading us to one village after another was confusing. Sometimes I was certain that we were going around in circles. We would take a road, go through some villages, and determine we were on the wrong road, so we would turn back to the original point and take another road.

On a wider road, we came to a full stop. First, we saw a dog walking straight toward us, and then further back we saw the sheep. They were coming back from grazing on a nearby pasture. We heard the bells ringing around their neck; we waved at the shepherd who smiled and raised his hand in salute. The sheep merged into one lane (carpool!) and passed us… we laughed at nature's "traffic" jam!

Papingo

We got to our destination, Papingo (accent on the Pah). There is Big Papingo and Little Papingo which are on the same road, one just past the other. They are considered to be the key villages that are popular destinations. Monasteries and churches abound as are quaint homes. We got there, but once again, due to lockdown, places were not open; we turned around and headed home.

Come Here Often?

What I found most interesting about this mountainous area were the numerous hotels – from small pensions to larger city-style buildings. This must mean that many people come here to rest and commune with nature. Once you get over the climb, you find yourself in a little bit of heaven on earth.

CORFU

Originally Published:

May 5, 2021

A ferry ride away from Ighoumenitsa, just west of Ioannina where we stayed last, is the beautiful island of Corfu AKA Kerkyra in Greek. We arrived mid-day and with the map in hand, we drove to our hotel going south to an area called Perama. Driving along the curves along the blue Ionian Sea showed us various places we made note of to come back and take photos – tired as we were, we drove on.

No Place At The Inn

Our hotel looked lovely – the only problem was that it was closed! Looking through the windows, we saw signs of renovations taking place and not a soul in sight. I called the number on our confirmation and a young man told me they were not ready to receive guests. I explained that we had made a reservation through a popular booking site and he apologized profusely. He asked if he could help us in any way; I said no, we would just drive around until we found somewhere else to stay. We turned around and headed back to Corfu Town, the center of the island. I did call him back the next day to make sure we were not charged; he assured me that we were not and then became totally adamant on how he wanted to help us find good accommodations or anything else we needed – he apologized profusely once again and gave us warm regards for a wonderful stay in Greece. A very nice young man indeed.

Memories

I remembered that over four decades ago, my two young friends and I stayed in an area called Dassia where we partied with people from all over the world! With a vague idea of where it was and confirmed when I saw it on the map, we headed towards it. We spotted an open hotel but decided to keep going up towards the beach. Numerous beautiful hotels are all over this area – alas, they were closed, so we went back to the open hotel we saw previously and checked in. Very nice, very comfortable, and very hospitable people. With that out of the way, we planned our days.

One of our outings was locating the exact spot of the hotel and restaurant with a pier from all those years ago. It was hard to find as much has changed; hotels and homes have been built, and memory can be faulty – but eureka! A sense of déjà vu came over me as we went through little dirt roads and between the trees; we found it! A flood of memories came flooding back as I pointed to different spots along the beach and told Zaf the stories of that summer in Dassia.

Antiquity

History tells us that Corfu dates back to 775-750 B.C. The Roman and the Byzantine Empires had strongholds here and faded away with the Norman conquest in 1081. Corfu overthrew them, with the help of the Venetian Fleet in 1149. The Venetians ruled here for over 200 years, hence the heavy Venetian influence in the architecture and the early political structure, leading it to be called the "Door to Venice." Then came the French followed by the British, all leaving their imprint on this international island.

The two fortresses here – the old and the new – both date back to antiquity from before Homer's time and were used to defend the inhabitants of this island from Ottoman Rule. The Old Town is situated between them and is a wonder to behold – we drove and walked through the streets, the wide plazas, the university and the library buildings, the archways, and stone-filled alleys. We talked about how it must have been to live here during these ancient times in these glorious buildings among such beauty.

Pastels

Stately three and four-story homes and buildings in various shades of dusty rose, pink, mauve, lavender, violet, and lilac abound; strong, bold doors with intricate wrought iron railings around them and on the balconies above reflect the wealth of the owners. The parks and public squares near the fortresses are surrounded by colleges, libraries, and government buildings – also resplendent in their size and color.

Throughout the island, even in tiny towns, these spring colors are the perfect setting among nature's greenery and the pure, crystal blue of the Ionian Sea. Intermingled throughout is an abundance of Wisteria – on homes, on trellises, on top of shops, along the road, at the front gate of hotels, and my personal favorite - on the archways leading into sweet gardens filled with flowers and vegetables. The color of this plant fits in perfectly with the pastels you see all around the island.

Touring

We spent our mornings driving from one end of the island to the other. Most of the roads are modern and fast, but we often went off-road into small villages, secluded beaches, and towns built way up in the mountains. Everywhere we went the vistas were glorious… there is not a place on this island where you don't have a view. It could be a simple spot between the trees looking down at copper rooftops of the homes and teeny cobblestone trees; it could be a wide expanse of sand and beach; it could be the mountain top with a little white chapel on it. The roads slope up and down the mountains and through farms and beach towns… we covered every inch of Corfu and will remember it all!

THIS IS WHERE WE LIVE NOW

Originally Published:

May 7, 2021

Ever live out of a suitcase? It can be both liberating and frustrating at the same time. After we sold our home and before we left for Greece, we lived in rental homes; not too bad as we were able to settle in and "pretend" we were at home. We had a living room and dining area, a kitchen, a bedroom, and a bathroom. Our clothes were in a bureau and a closet; we had a washing machine and a dryer. We even had a lovely garden to sit in.

And yet… we felt transitory.

Any Day Now

Knowing that we had tickets to Greece kept us from really hunkering down. Each day was a step forward towards our departure to our Retirement Kickoff! We did not buy long-term things such as toilet paper or water; we bought just enough to see us through the few weeks before we left. It felt "cozy" but alienating at the same time because we could see our "Greek" suitcases standing in the corner every day. At times, with deep sighs, we could hardly contain ourselves about how we were living; it seemed stifling at best.

Epiphany

The day came, however, that I realized that we chose to live this way. We didn't count on being "in town" for more than a few weeks, so when we had to spend two and a half months in a rental, it was a bit of a let-down. Once I grasped the notion that this is simply where we live now… and how we would be living for the next seven to eight months, our perspective and mood changed. I told Zaf: "We need to get used to this suitcase thing as this is how it is going to be throughout Greece as we travel from place to place." This lightened us up and gave us clarity as to how and why we decided to do this.

Reminder

Two years ago, we decided to retire in 2021. We picked February 28th, 2021 as the day to pull the plug and hit the road. The Road to Greece. Both of us, being born there and growing up in strong Greek homes, we wanted to reconnect with our roots and spend time there among our family, friends, home-towns, ancient ruins, the unbelievable light of the Grecian sun, and the crystal blue waters of the Aegean and the Ionian Seas.

Good Habits

Because we got into a good rhythm of suitcase living in the USA, it proved to be a good step forward as we arrived in Athens and checked into a hotel for a few days set the tone. Zaf likes to hang up some of his clothes and put others in drawers. His shoes line up on the closet floor and his toiletry kit is on the bathroom cabinet.

My choice is to have the most needed items on the top of the open suitcase and hang up just what needs to be hung up. Some shoes are on the closet floor; some are in the suitcase. It might be because I have so much more than he does, or it might be because Zaf is slightly more neurotic about his stuff. Not sure – am leaning towards the neatnik mentality though, as I know myself pretty well. I am tidy of course, but at the end of the day, my pants might just be left on the back of a chair while they are already folded at the crease and hung up…. honestly!

Pare Down

We knew we over-packed right from the get-go. It was confirmed at the airport when we paid hundreds of dollars in overweight charges…. but we planned to be gone for six months - we kept saying to ourselves!

While at the hotel in Salonika, we outlined our next venture to see Greece; we knew we would be gone over five weeks, including Greek Orthodox Easter, so we analyzed our needs. By then, we discovered that hey! – we can buy toothpaste and mouthwash at the local supermarket! We packed up two of the smaller suitcases with "stuff" and left them at the hotel – where we would be returning to. A bit more expensive than normal to buy most of these toiletries, but worth every penny not to lug it around.

Living through it now, after traveling for three and a half weeks as of today, we can see how we can pare down even more. Waiting for the warmer weather to begin, we don't need the heavier sweaters and pants; we can leave those back at the hotel as we frolic on the beaches of the beautiful blue sea!

Retirement Living

Our days here have created a rhythm of their own, and the repetition of it brings comfort. I wake up early and head down to the lobby for my first cup of coffee. A robe over pajamas, with hotel key in hand, I say Kalee Merah (Good Morning) to the staff as they hand me the cup. After their first day, they know I'll be down early and have it ready for me!

Upstairs, we clean up, get dressed, and head back down for breakfast. It is typical for hotels to provide breakfast; in some cases, you can book a room without breakfast for a less expensive price, but who wants to scrounge around looking for a coffee shop at 7:00am – especially during lockdown and especially in my pajamas!

We head out for a long walk and some window shopping; right now, the lockdown still prevents us from going into the stores. Sometimes we drive to another part of the town or island and see the sights. Around 1:00pm, we stop and grab some lunch which we eat on a bench outside the shop, in tucked away gazebos, or by the bay.

Back at the hotel, the best thing ever created in the universe awaits us – the Siesta! I nap, and Zaf fiddles with his computer. Quiet ensues throughout the land. At 4:30 – 5:00pm, the first sights and sounds stir us up again for the evening schedule; we take another walk, pick up dessert, and head back to the hotel where we order in and eat in the lounge. Typically, other guests and/or the owner of the hotel start up a conversation and we get to have some interesting exchanges of thoughts and opinions about everything going on in the world. Without the lockdown, we would be going to local tavernas for our meals – but we are willing to wait another week or so to do this so we can relive Greece as we knew it before!

It does get a bit boring on the days when rain keeps us indoors, but we sneak out between downpours for short walks. This emphasizes the point that we need to have things to do inside the house to keep us busy when we return home; I blog and organize my photos as well as my online work, but Zaf will be challenged. After all, how much puttering can he do in the garage!?

When I think about it, this will probably be the same rhythm of our lives once we are back home and in our new house. A bit of activity in the morning – chores, errands, and a bit of work for me. Then lunch and some quiet time. Dinner on the back patio or with friends or out at a local restaurant. Our being here and getting this pattern in motion is very good practice for the future because, after all, this is where we live now.

PARGA, PREVEZA, PATRAS

Originally Published:

May 10, 2021

After our five-day stay in Corfu, we loaded the car and set off to other parts of Greece. Our ultimate goal was to another beautiful island on the Ionian Sea. There was no connection from Corfu so the ferry took us back onto the mainland; we followed the coast south to Parga. The photos I've seen of Parga were of a pretty coastal town on the western coastline, so we headed down that way. Curvy roads took us there and the first sight of this town was picture-perfect. Once again, the hotel we booked on that same online booking site, proved to be closed. And once again, the owner was kind enough to call us and tell us of a B&B that was open and would be able to take us in.

Settling In

We got to the B&B after crawling up tiny roads where we had to back out three times because there was no room for us to move forward. People here drive tiny cars! An old lady saw us – Zaf inching his way forward as I walked along the car searching for this place – she guided us towards it, and the hostess just happened to be outside. She greeted us warmly and her husband ran out to help with the suitcases. We climbed the stairs into a lovely room with a modern kitchen and bath that was very accommodating. The refrigerator was filled with breakfast fare – eggs, cheese, ham, butter, marmalade, sliced bread – as well as orange juice, water, beer and wine. The cabinets had coffee, tea, and all the fixings. A large bowl of fresh fruit was on the counter. Each morning, the hostess knocked on the door and brought us freshly baked breakfast bread. The large balcony was the perfect sight for our dinner delivery as well as hanging out and breathing the fresh, clean air.

Parga

Parga has two coves, so we drove to each one and admired the beach, the sea, and the lovely homes once again built up against the mountains. A large waterfront allows for good healthy walks as we browsed in the few shops that were open. The Kastro loomed high over the cove as it stood guard over the town. One day it rained, so we stayed in our room and balcony. By early evening, the rain was coming down hard; thunder boomed and lightning struck! We played cards on the balcony and laughed through it all. We left with a promise to return to this charming little place; about ten minutes out we got a phone call from the host asking if we mistakenly took the key with us. Yikes! I did… we told him we'll bring it back. Once we got there again, the hostess was waiting with another handful of breakfast bread she made for us for our trip. Such wonderful, gracious people!

Preveza

A big town – unexpected. It has large streets with an abundance of stores and office buildings, a fairly large port, and a charming waterfront strand. We drove through it and stayed on course going south along the water.

Veering inland for about twenty minutes, we got to the monument of Zalongo. Up, up, up into the mountains to a forested area, a monastery is tucked away barely visible until close up. We did not enter as we had been here before. The monument of about 300 women who fell to their deaths to avoid abuse, slavery, or slaughter from the Ottoman enemy, carrying their children in their arms, is right above us on the mountain cliff; when we last saw it, it was being renovated. I was told by a nearby villager that two baby girls survived. And now it proudly stands as a testament to the call of Independence: Freedom or Death. The famous song commemorating this event was danced to by me and my classmates while in Greek school so many decades ago. Every Greek child learns about these brave women as part of our history.

Patras

When I say: "We got to Rio" you probably think I'm talking about the city in Brazil, but I'm not. Rio is the name of the bridge that connects mainland Greece to the Peloponnese Peninsula. Just past Messolonghi, where Lord Byron died in a massive battle fighting for Greece's independence, you see the bridge from a distance. This area of Greece is full of history and sits as Greece's most important sea link with the rest of Europe.

Crossing under the steel vertical arches is one of my favorite things to do; we've done this a number of times and it is always awe-inspiring. Some people even choose to walk across on the pedestrian walkway! We get across into the town of Patras: Greece's third-largest city. We got lost here one time, so now we know to avoid the center of town; we headed south once again, hugging the sea.

We Got The Ferry!

What looks like a short distance on the map sometimes takes longer than expected, especially after being in the car since early morning; it was now late afternoon. Signage is often confusing. They'll post the name of the town that comes AFTER the town you want, so if you didn't know that name, you had no idea if you were going the right way or not. Once or twice, we asked for directions and thankfully we were. Slight rain didn't help. To say that we were concerned that we would miss the ferry would be a true understatement. Finally, after about an hour and a half, the signs to our destination materialized and we got to Killini, the port town where ferries go back and forth to our next stop: Kefalonia.

Retirement exploring can be fun, can be interesting, can be nail-biting – just the way we like it!

KEFALONIA

Originally Published:

May 17, 2021

One of the seven glorious islands in the Ionian Sea. Our ferry ride from Killini, on the west side of the Peloponnese, took about three hours and we disembarked in Poros, at the southeast port of the island. We selected this particular island for two reasons: one is because we had visited once before and only saw a tiny bit of it at the very top and two, my late brother-in-law Jerry's father was born here and we wanted to visit in his honor.

The Bus Route

Once out of the port, the signage becomes negligible at best so we took some side streets that led us to one village after another; finally, I spotted a bus heading up the mountain and thought – well, the people who came off the ferry and then got on the bus, had to be heading to some city – so I said to Zaf, FOLLOW THE BUS! We did, through mountain turn after mountain turn, along the blue, blue sea, and of course the numerous red-tiled houses of little villages tucked in between. And yes, the bus took us to the very place we wanted to go.

Argostoli

The capital of Kefalonia is the city called Argostoli. If there ever was a very well-laid-out city, this is it! On the west side of the island, in a gulf where it faces the water and the mountains beyond, this pretty city lives. The shoreline is dotted with restaurants and cafes, fresh vegetable markets and flower stands, fishermen crying out the names of the fish they caught that morning, and lots of benches on the strand where we sat and had lunch while enjoying the scenery. Retirement life is good!

Myrtos Beach

A mile and a half long, in a perfect arc shape, this beach is probably the most photographed in all of Greece. Voted continuously as one of the most beautiful beaches of the world… and yes, it really does have three shades of blue from the shoreline to the deepest part. It is located in Divarata, the hometown of Jerry's father. While we could not actually go down the road to the beach itself (lockdown!), we were able to see it from the top of the road where we stopped to have our "lemonada."

Ithaka

We decided to have our own Odyssey and find our way to Ithaka. In Greek: EETHAKEE – with the accent on the second EE. Driving up and through the mountains to the other side of Argostoli, we got to the port town of Sami. Here is one of the places where we were stopped by the authorities; the big guy in charge. In a white cap and double-breasted blue jacket with lots of gold buttons (surrounded by his minions), he asked for our papers and reminded us that Greece was under lockdown. I replied by telling him that we knew all about the lockdown and yet we have been allowed to travel all over Greece since March 22nd. He was shocked! He shook his head, then smiled (tightly) and told us to "Enjoy Greece!"

We drove around and found the lovely city of Vathee. We ate a bit of lunch at the large town square in the cove where we sat next to the statue of Odysseus. This is the place where he struggled for ten years to return to after the Trojan War. We now understand why Homer chose this island for the determined and relentless struggle to return to his homeland – it is indeed the most beautiful place. We are amazed and oh so proud that history and mythology surround us, not only here, but all over Greece.

The funny thing that happened when we returned to the port of Sami, one of the minions spotted us and called out, "Ah, the Americans came back!!!" We waved at him gleefully.

Prayers

On our second day there, we celebrated the Eastern Orthodox Palm Sunday. A lovely church was just minutes away from our hotel; we entered and lit some candles. A little old lady waved at me and pointed to some side seats that were available; I nodded my head (I also smiled but who can see behind the stupid masks we are all wearing). We gave thanks for bringing us back to our birth country and for the amazing travel we experienced so far. Our adorned palms given to us as we entered the church are safely tucked away in our suitcases so they can come back with us.

Next Stop

We drove back down to Poros and took the ferry back to Killini, then up to the Rio Bridge and across the Korinthiakos Gulf to Nafpaktos, one of our favorite small towns in all of Greece.

Exploring Greece in our retirement is a dream come true, and we are retiring well.

NAFPAKTOS

Originally Published:

May 28, 2021

This is our third visit to Nafpaktos because we absolutely love it! Small enough to be able to travel around effortlessly and big enough to provide a bustling environment filled with shops, restaurants, and sites to see. And of course, where our dear friends Alecko and Tasoula live.

Harbor

This pretty city is situated on a lovely bay with a walled harbor which seems to be the center of town where everyone gathers, especially the young people who sit on the low wall and drink endless amounts of coffee.

Venetian Castle

Just a short ride up the mountainside brings you to a magnificent Venetian Castle offering great views of the little hamlets below, the harbor, and all of Nafpaktos. Originally built in the fifth century, it was fortified during the Venetian period of occupancy. Just as you are climbing up into the castle, a taverna sits on your left side, built up against the castle, with yet again amazing views. Great to have drinks there in the late afternoon, dinner at sunset, and nightcaps to watch the stars.

Shoreline

On either side of the harbor are two long stretches of beaches and a walking strand for miles and miles. All of this gives you an incredible vista of Patra across the two gulfs – the Korinthiakos and the Patraikos which are separated by the glorious Rio Bridge. Restaurants and cafes abound on the strand; it is hard to choose from as they offer an incredible array of food, most notably the fresh fish caught that day. Numerous hotels face the shoreline… rooms with windows that open up to a larger expanse of the water, the bridge, and the surrounding mountains.

Monasteries

On a previous trip to Nafpaktos, Alecko and Tasoula drove us up to the highest point of a nearby mountain to an incredible monastery. The buildings there date back hundreds of years and are situated on a large plot of land where numerous buildings are built containing chapels, offices, and the dorms where the monks live. They have a museum and gift shop as well. On the property itself, you find goats, chickens, and a variety of other animals. Just beyond, there are numerous fruit trees and a large vegetable garden.

An entire area has been created as a day camp for children to spend time with the animals, learn how to garden, and just have fun! A peaceful area is set further back where a little creek meanders under little bridges where you can walk across and see the other side of the mountain – another vista that amazes you.

The most notable feature here are the little niches portraying different aspects of the Eastern Orthodox Faith such as Jesus as a baby, the Virgin Mary, and other saints. The most notable of all is a large – very large – free-standing wall composed of thirty large niches containing bells. These bells are rung on the most holiest days of the Orthodox calendar. It is a remarkable sight to behold.

Our next stop, as we descended the mountain, was another monastery for nuns. We were allowed access and we went through chapels and small, quiet areas set aside for moments of reflection. And then, we entered the catacombs. These were built as replicas of the real catacombs that existed when Greece was occupied by foreign nations; churches and schools went underground to preserve them. And so they did, through hundreds of years which thrive in Greece today. Here is a photo of Zaf going through the tiny catacomb openings From The Personal Collection of Helene and Zaf.

Easter

Our dream was to spend Resurrection services at the monastery so we could hear the bells chime at midnight. Alas, due to restrictions, we were unable to do so. It would have been absolutely marvelous to hear them ring out in glory! We spent Holy Friday night services at the Harbor amidst a crowd of people awaiting the shining cross to appear over the water. When it did, a sense of peace and wonder was felt by all. We walked back to our hotel in reverence. Saturday night, we got to the church and sat in silence as the prayers were read; we then followed the procession outside where the prayers continued until the Light was given to us that proclaimed that truly He has risen! Amazing to be surrounded by those who truly believed as fireworks exploded in celebration.

Weekenders

This town is a popular place for a weekend trip as it is not too far from Athens and Ioannina. The drive from either place is doable in a few hours with roads that are very good. A large number of people who originally hail from this part of the country still have homes here that they have modernized and now serve as the perfect getaway. If only we lived close by, we would be here every weekend!

Retirement joy is not only experiencing new places but returning to the ones we love again and again!

NAFPLION

Originally Published:

June 14, 2021

This former capital of Greece (1821-1834) has retained its charm and beauty over the centuries. Old Town bustles with tiny shops filled with clothes, shoes, jewelry, leather sandals, purses, groceries, etc. I counted three shops that display hand-made worry beads in all sizes and colors, and they offer to repair the ones you have. Gentle squares open up with restaurants all around them so grown-ups can watch the children play in the central area as they drink their kafe; the streets are cobblestoned and lead you all around in a maze. All of this is under the watchful eye of the massive Castle/Kastro. A smaller Kastro sits in the middle of the bay; it's awesome to stand in one Kasto and look at the other.

Kastro Sweet Kastro

Our directions to the hotel were once again a bit hazy; we asked for assistance and followed the turns that led us up to the halfway point of the Kastro. No Hotel In Sight! We circled back down again and called; the owner told us to come back up to where we stopped, and he would meet us there. Once there, we parked and his very welcoming greeting included pointing down a series of steps, under an archway, and another series of long steps (oh, my back!).

Once we turned the corner, it all fell into place. A very large and comfortable room awaited us overlooking Old Town and the sea beyond. The view outside our window was amazing! The owner brought in the luggage and we settled in. Zaf offered to go to Old Town to pick up some water and fruit. He followed the owner's suggestion of using the steps on the side of the hotel to get to the shops. He took a long time to come back, and I got worried. Finally, he arrived totally out of breath – he gasped, "There has to be about 80 steps out there!" While the hotel is lovely as it has several rooms on various levels up and down the side of the Kastro and a rooftop dining area with beautiful views of the water and boats moored there, we determined that climbing back up to the main road and driving down is our best option!

Mycenae

Just a short drive from the center of Nauplio is the ancient Citadel of Mycenae. From about 1600 BC to 11 BC, the Mycenaen civilization was a very important part of Greek history. Walking through the remnants of this archeological site, it was easy to imagine how the rooms were set up and what area was set up for different functions.

Again, the stairs/walking is a bit long but very worth the effort. Wear a hat, lots of sunscreen, and comfortable walking shoes. Check out the museum – absolutely amazing pieces of bronze age artifacts… we saw some unbelievable jewelry!

Restaurant Row

Down by port, there is a whole series of restaurants; it was hard to choose. We typically choose one based on how it looks. Color of table cloths, styles of chairs, umbrellas – sometimes Zaf picks and sometimes I do. One day, I picked the name of the place. The Pine Tree – because it reminded me of the trees in my parents' villages. The food was incredibly delicious as I knew it would be! When we were there, it was early in the season and with just coming out of the lockdown, the menus were often limited. But we made do with lamb chops, lemon potatoes, calamari, octopus, Greek village salad, cheese pies and spinach pies, moussaka, pastichio, and of course, ice cream or baklava or kataiifi – you got the picture, right?!

Coastline

The ride out of town took us through the typical city center with all the shopping you need to do and then down the coast to our next exploration. We were originally planning to take the "main road" (highway) traveling south into the Peloponnese but Petros, our hotel host, insisted we take the shoreline. We were happy we did…. unbelievable vistas of the sea with its myriad of coves and bays, cliffs and hamlets tucked into the hills. We stopped at Leonidio – a good-sized town and took the path down to the beach. We chose a tiny taverna to have our lunch, fed some cats, and took off again climbing the central mountains towards Sparta.

MYSTRAS – MONEMVASIA

Originally Published:

June 18, 2021

Mystras is tucked away in the mountainside just outside of Sparta (Sparti in Greek). This is our second visit here as we thoroughly enjoyed the coolness of the mountains in a quaint little town.

Mystras

On our first trip here, we just meandered in; I read about this place and saw some photos. I just knew we had to see it in person. The sweet village square is really tiny; you can see the entire place from just standing still right in the middle of it. Three restaurants, two hotels, a couple of grocery stores, and a souvenir shop. But then, when you get back into the car, drive to the right, and follow the road, up you go! Just a little ways up sits a taverna which has good food and a great view of all of Sparti. We met the owners last time we were there in 2014, and once they figured out who we were again, a warm welcome was received. The owner sat with us throughout the entire meal, and we had a wonderful evening talking about our two cultures. She had lived in the US for many years. The most notable part of this taverna is that it is built into the castle and has been there since 1890. Continuing past the taverna are winding mountain roads leading to small villages; one in particular, we stayed at last time and it was an incredible find. Not a hotel as we know it, but a series of luxurious cottages overseeing the entire valley with excellent service. Alas, it was not open at this time.

Mystras Castle

Built in the 1200's, this castle is just the beginning of a series of buildings that go into the Taygetus mountain range and proved to be quite steep. We only climbed about halfway up because honestly, I just couldn't do it anymore! But what we did was absolutely amazing. Monasteries, churches, and fortress walls all intertwined in a rocky, rugged landscape with stone walkways and stairs – good grief! Those stairs are endless! At the very top is the palace, naturally. That is something that we did not get to see close up as it was truly too far to climb. This is an incredible place worth seeing - even if you are like me and can only climb so far!

Monemvasia

Leaving Mystras, we drove down the Peloponnese ever further heading southeast towards the Aegean ocean. Not too bad of a ride as the mountains were not too high and the roads were good, except for going through the town where for some unknown reason, the roads get narrower! Finally, we got to the shoreline and followed it down to the city of Monemvasia. Once there, you take the causeway and drive to the Kastro. Here the entire island is an immense rock formation; the Kastro is built on the south side, and you can only drive as far as the gate. When we got there, the only available parking was back down near the causeway, and it is a long way back up on foot!

Our hotel was amazing; you climb a series of stone steps into a foyer which is the reception area with the dining area located off to the left and just beyond that is an outdoor terrace. Because you can't drive into the kastro, the staff comes down to the gate to pick up your luggage and deliver it to your room. We climb another series of steps inside the hotel into a truly beautiful room. First, a foyer with a loft to our left and a modern bathroom. A beautiful, large bedroom awaited us with a sitting area, a fireplace, and windows leading out to a view of the sea on one side and the red-tiled buildings on the other side. A private patio was accessible from our bedroom and from our foyer, so Zaf was able to sleep in while I snuck out for my early morning coffee which was delivered with a discreet knock on the door.

Walking back down to the cobblestone road, we encountered shops on both sides showcasing jewelry, clothing, souvenirs, and restaurants. It is the only road where these things are located as the rest of the town has small alleys and paths leading to the homes of the residents there and some lookout points. Everything is built into the Kastro on various levels intertwining with steps, arches, and ancient stone structures. The Kastro is quite large and high – you can walk through it and up to nearly the top where the churches are located. We did not climb there as it is not an easy trek for those of us who are not hearty hikers. Our meals were on rooftops of the few restaurants open at this time – all giving us an expansive view of the sea; small boats floated by as we watched the sunset each evening.

This magical place has been on our bucket list for a long time, and we are forever grateful that we planned to spend a few days here enjoying the walk back to antiquity and the surrounding blue water. We left with high spirits that we saw this glorious place although we had to head back to Mystras because Zaf left some of his clothes back at that hotel! We zipped in, and those lovely people had them all in a bag for us. We zipped right out again towards our next destination.

Retirement is what you make of it, and we are doing what we can to make ours exploring a series of wonderful memories!

MY SECOND DREAM COMES TRUE IN TUSCANY

Originally Published:

June 21, 2021

As you all probably know from reading my blog, our first dream was to spend a length of time in Greece. Well, our second dream was to visit Tuscany. I've been in love with all things Italian since I was a little girl; I've been to Italy three times before but never explored the famous vineyards of Tuscany. So, off we went for a twelve-day tour.

Long Day

We began our journey with an early morning airplane ride from Thessaloniki to Athens and then on to Rome. From there, a cab ride to the Rome Termini train station, a train ride to Florence where we picked up a local train – making endless stops – to Lucca where we arrived at 11:30pm! We fell into a deep sleep and woke up to a dream come true.

Lucca

Much has been said about Florence, and it is indeed the center of the Renaissance, but Lucca is in a category of its own. A walled city that is simply beautiful. Small and large streets inter-connecting at various points into piazzas where churches, towers, and tall statues can be found. Along the way, restaurants and cafes spill out into the streets under arches and trees and tucked away in alleys.

The Antitheatro, formally a coliseum, is huge. While it has a big open arena in the middle, all around are restaurants and little shops. We ate there a couple of times, but our favorite places were those where the locals ate outside in the off streets; we met an American couple at lunch one day who live there full time now! They gave us the names of a few places, and we tried them – they were the best!

During the day, you see the locals going to work or errands, lingering at cafes, or just walking around. Siesta time brings a lull to activity only to spring into full bloom at about 6:00pm when it seems like the whole town has locked its doors and filled the streets. They were seen popping in and out of the numerous shops, ordering espressos while standing on the sidewalk beside the counters or taking long walks. By 8:00pm, the restaurants were filled; on several occasions, we could not be seated because the tables were all reserved. Young people congregated in certain sections where the noise level was quite high with chatter and laughter; older people had their own areas where they met up with family and friends.

A carousel was just outside our hotel where you could hear the laughter of children as they came around. The entirety of Lucca came alive; it was as though they had to get their evening packed with merriment before curfew struck at 10:00pm. They didn't want to waste one single minute. I fell in love with Lucca.

Barga

Outside of Lucca, about half an hour away by car, is the town of Barga; another charming city, much smaller but lovely in its own way. Just outside of it was our destination hotel high up in the mountains.

A first-class hotel with all the best amenities and views you can imagine. We took a taxi here, and since we did not have our own car, we were limited to taking rides into the green surrounding landscape. Other than a day's trip into the town of Barga, we relaxed and enjoyed the scenery. One early morning, I drew back the curtains and I saw this:

The cloud formation hovered over the valley that lingered for a couple of hours. It is an amazing sight to see, and I just had to capture it to share it with you. Our exploration has given us unforgettable sights indeed!

We went back to Lucca for a few more days and then onto Florence.

Florence

My third trip to Florence did not disappoint. And while Zaf and I had visited the key points on a previous trip, we made sure we covered the spots we missed. A Uffizi museum tour, an inside peek of the Duomo (we turned down the opportunity to climb over 460 steps to the top!), and a day trip to Pisa where we also turned down the opportunity to climb over 295 steps to the top! A return visit to Ponte Vecchio, browsing at the outdoor flea markets, and lunch at the Mercado Central were one day's excursions. Zaf bought two leather belts, and I bought a beautiful leather bag which I carried back to Greece in a shopping bag because I just couldn't seem to let it go out of my hand!

Retirement Highlight!

We booked a private eight-hour tour of Siena, San Gimignano, Monteriggioni, and the Chianti Vineyards. Our driver, Alejandro, picked us up at the hotel, and off we went. A fountain of knowledge, he began by telling us some historical facts about the wine country. He spoke perfect English and indeed was fluent in seven languages! After about an hour, we arrived in Siena. I can't begin to tell you how beautiful and astounding this place is. We walked into the walled town through a stone arch and began our walk through cobblestone streets interspersed with alleyways and steps leading to other streets curving around and around the town.

The main piazza is quite large; in ancient times, they held horse races here. The horses ran around the entire circle (which is identified), and everyone stood in the middle of the circle. There was betting and much fighting with punches thrown for good measure. The antiquity of this place is mind-boggling (and we come from an even more ancient birthplace!). If you take a minute to really look at the old stone homes and other structures, you can picture the citizens of the past walking through here, mingling with the merchants and the farmers who came into town to sell their crops. This place is in stiff competition with Lucca as my favorite place in Tuscany.

With much reluctance, we left for San Gimignano. Once again, we drove up to the gate of the walled city. This time, we walked into a medieval city! The churches, the towers, the piazzas, and the complicated little streets leading to other complicated little streets were spellbinding. Lunch at the main square gave us time and opportunity to watch people, and while we spotted a few tourists here and there, our focus was on the locals who actually live here. A small-town feel where everyone knew each other; a delivery truck pulled up to drop off products to not just one store but to many of the stores in the square. Talking loudly, waving their hands, borrowing boxes and barrels from one another, and shouting Ciao, Ciao as they drove away made our day!

Vineyards

I had told Alejandro that, for me, Tuscany was vineyards upon vineyards. And so, we were given a tour of a lifetime. Through the area of Monteriggioni and then through Chianii, we climbed hill after hill with views of one vineyard after another. Of course, this time of year, they were not fully grown, but nevertheless, they were there. Greenery all around, lanes leading from one hill to another; we could not get enough of viewing the vistas from the top of the hills all the way to the bottom. And then he drove us into Chianti Supiriori. This is the more elite area which is identified by the land structure of vineyard ownership and their vineyards.

The owner lived at the top of the hill in a villa – naturally! The immediate landscape was the garden and stoned patios overlooking the entire property. Some smaller homes stood a little further away, and that is where the staff lived. From that point on, as far as you can see, were the vineyards. Rows and rows, symmetrical in size and shape, there they were… the vines that grew the grapes were harvested in the fall and thus made wine. We stopped at a private vineyard (Alejandro has connections!) and took our photos. I began to cry, so overwhelmed by the fact that I was actually here.

Florence Again

Our leisurely drive back to Florence took the long route home; we drove through the outskirts to see some very upscale neighborhoods and some not so nice; we stopped at the David Statue piazza high above Florence with a magnificent view of the entire city; we drove through the center of town once again and arrived back at our hotel. A tad expensive, but worth every Euro.

Retirement can bring in some new experiences you've wanted to have for years and years. That is a good thing; it can also bring you back to some places where you have been before but now can see with a fresh, new perspective, and that is a good thing too!

KALO DROMO

Originally Published:

July 2, 2021

Good Road… this is the one phrase we have heard over and over again here in Greece. It is a wish for your journey ahead. And since we are on our Retirement Journey – it fits right in with how we are kicking off our retirement with a six-month stay in Greece.

Everyone we come in contact with from the hotel staff, the restaurant staff, the people in the kiosks, the shop owners, the toll booth people, etc. say this to us wishing us well on our travels ahead. The open-heartedness of this expression is given with warmth and sincerity. The Greeks love their tourists and want us to enjoy their country which we are definitely doing.

Hitting the Road

Kalo Dromo to us also means ROAD TRIP! We have traveled all over Greece in a rental car going through mountains and tunnels, over bridges large and small, into small towns curving our way to each destination. The National Roads are excellent; they are in good condition with clear signage of where we are and where we want to go. The rest areas are numerous – offering food and drinks, bathrooms, outdoor sitting areas, and some have shops as well. All are clean and comfortable. Typically, the gas station is right next door so you can fill up as well, and off you go!

The secondary roads are also good, most of them are asphalt with some minor exceptions where it is still gravel in smaller, more rural areas. Then we have the country/local roads (in some cases they are called the old roads) which is where the fun begins!

These old roads have proven to be the best experience for us. Tiny, twisting lanes have led us down to beautiful little coves with tiny tavernas offering the fresh catch of the day as we watch the local fisherman in his boat.

Sometimes it can be a little hairy, where a road suddenly ends and there is hardly any room for us to turn around! Zaf has become a master U-turn driver! Exploring is what Zaf and I enjoy the most as it takes us away from the typical crowded places where tourists go. We like seeing inner Greece where the people who work the fields and tend the sheep live and work. It is said to note that this is the side most tourists don't see, which is unfortunate.

Unexpected

One time, on a previous trip, as we crossed a little bridge, high in the mountains of central Greece, right across from a little white church stood a little house-like structure. My cousin told us to stop there for some delicious meatballs. From the outside, it didn't look like much, but we took a chance. Walking up to what was a little patio, conversation stopped all around. I walked into a little sitting area with a kitchen attached; a woman looked up at me in distress… she knew I was a foreigner, but she didn't speak any other language but Greek. I smiled and said to her in Greek, "I heard you had delicious meatballs." She burst out laughing and waved her hands in the air inviting me in… I told her my husband was outside so she rushed out and told her husband that we were Greek!

The chairs were pulled out, a white tablecloth appeared, and we sat down. We ordered and the questions started flying… Where were we from? What were we doing here? Not only from the owners of the restaurant but from everyone on the patio! I told them my parents came from the surrounding villages and that we were on our way there to see the ancestral homes. We ate well, paid the bill, and bid them Yiassou! They said Kalo Dromo. The beer was on the house!

OPA!

As we were driving along, I fiddled with the radio and found a station that plays Greek music from our own generation as well as modern hits. We played it loud to the amusement of the toll booth people when Zaf rolls down the window to pay. I dance in my seat, waving my arms and snapping my fingers, to the amusement of the truck drivers who can see me from where they sit. We drive through the beautiful country, sometimes singing along, enjoying the fact that we are there!

Why Me?

I just want to point out that no matter what direction we go in, the sun is always on my side. My right arm is typically draped by a light sweater to keep the sun's rays away. No matter how much sunscreen I use, I have to cover up. Once in a while, my feet are in the sun as well, so another sweater has to go there. I can't figure it out, but I think sometimes Zaf is doing it on purpose!

Good Continuation

Another expression said often is Kalee Sinehia (see-neh-hia) which means good continuation or good progress. They want us to enjoy every single moment ahead and wish us well as we drive on to our next destination. Sometimes we see them in the rear-view mirror as they wave yiassas (goodbye) to us!

It has really left an impression on us. Two simple phrases, given in good cheer, send us off to the next adventure with a warm and fuzzy feeling in our hearts. These moments are what travel is all about – connecting with other people who live in another country. Exploring our retirement is not just about monuments, museums, beaches and bridges. It is about humanity shining through.

PAROS – NAXOS – ANTIPAROS

Originally Published:

July 16, 2021

▬▬▬

I was really hesitant to write about these islands because I wanted to keep them all to myself! But, I am afraid that the word is already out about their absolute beauty so here is my contribution to our visit there.

Paros

If there was ever a place to kick back and totally relax, this is it! From the moment you disembark in the port town of Parikia, you begin to unwind and get into low gear. A lively port with one café after another as far as you can see, plus the Old Town where you can meander up and down stone streets and browse the various shops offering clothes, jewelry, household goods, souvenirs, beach wear, etc. We walked through these little streets and found ourselves climbing towards the fortress, but as we looked up the stairs to get to the gate, we decided, "Enough for us retired folks!" Several travel offices here give you choices for the next stops in the Aegean or back to the mainland. Word of caution: both going to and from Paros, we had to wait about five hours for the ferry after its original departure time! Worker strikes spring up when you least expect them!

We drove to our hotel about 15 minutes away from the port, just outside the town of Naoussa. Right on the water, a beautiful setting of whitewashed townhomes with balconies and a gorgeous pool surrounded by the bar and outside dining area completed the serenity we felt when we first got to the island. Speaking of whitewashed, it seems this is the favorite color here (almost everywhere in Greece, in fact!). Coupled with the "Greek" blue doors and windows, often tables and chairs in the tavernas too, it is indeed the images you see of Greece when on social media or when doing your own online search, or in the myriad of books and magazine articles about this truly "Blue" country – blue sky, blue waters, blue décor! Coupled with the white light of Greece – magical! We ate often down by the port watching the people strolling by and hearing the boats bumping and squeaking along the pier.

Reunion

Paros was on our bucket list of islands to visit, but when childhood friends reached out to me on social media saying they would be visiting here this summer, it made it more of a definite decision. Our first night, with one of the brothers and his family, was at a small but elegant restaurant in a tiny port about half an hour from our hotel going south.

Unbelievable that I can see my friend again after 35 years in the country of our heritage! Zaf and his family sat on one side of the table and kept their conversation going, knowing that my friend and I had much to talk about – about our childhood and all the memories we shared! And then, a few days later, his brother flew in and we got together at their beautiful villa where they prepared the most delicious dinner; we talked and laughed into the night! I'm so grateful we were able to connect after all these years!

Naxos

Speaking of day trips, we took the ferry once again in a different direction to the nearby island of Naxos. Upon arrival, we were greeted by Naxos Portara (The Great Door) – The Temple of Apollo. It got its name from the temple which faces the island of Delos believed to be the place where Apollo was born.

This island has a really terrific port – a long line of restaurants hugging the shoreline, a great strand for strolling, and tons of shops! It's quite pretty and a great place to sit, eat, and relax. The town of Naxos is yet another beautiful place with whitewashed buildings cascading down hills… the port is alive with cafes, restaurants, shops, and a magnificent view of the sea.

There are amazingly beautiful beaches along roads that are dotted with pretty towns and ancient ruins to be admired for their awesomeness. We are not "beach" people; we both get antsy after a bit and want to be on the move. So, we took a long drive and then enjoyed the walk through the old town and kastro and lunch at the port. Naxos is a haven for beach lovers!

Antiparos

Right at that tiny port in Paros where we had our reunion dinner, a little ferry took us across to Antiparos. A really small island with a delightful port with tavernas and shops. Intertwining cobblestone streets made up the little town there, and we had fun going down one street after another until we went to a street that was a dead end. We had to back out all the way down to the main road – maybe it would be a good idea to post a sign! We then drove to one end of this small island and saw the beautiful sea from several different spots. We then wound back to the port for a light lunch. A great day trip from Paros for us.

Overall, our retirement plans to explore restful, serene places definitely included these islands. The magic happens when you come here and look into the deep blue sea and feel young at heart!

LIVADIA – ARAHOVA – GALAXIDI

Originally Published:

July 30, 2021

For a complete change of pace from the beautiful Aegean isles, we ferried back to the port of Pireaus, just outside Athens, and drove several hours north to Livadia – our second trip there. Entering the city at 10pm was quiet and welcoming. Upon arriving, we happily stopped next door at a little taverna for our late dinner.

The next morning, we drove to one of the prettiest sights we've seen in Greece, so a quick drive to the other side of town was a must. A sight totally unexpected, as the city is just like the many others: narrow streets, shops and stores, and cafes on every corner. But, go past the center and head for the mountain behind it, and you will be greeted by a most beautiful stream where water cascades over rocks and foliage from one level to the next… all the way down and under the city. A mill, once a working enterprise, stands next to it and reminds us of how people used to live and work here. Conveniently, several cafes are located here so you can spend time admiring the beauty and relaxing in the cool shade of the glorious trees next to the streaming water.

Arahova

Definitely a must on my list. Arahova was a drive-through on our way to Delphi on our last trip, but it always stuck in my mind as a charming little town. A beautiful mountainous area with basically one big road where all the shops and restaurants are – but oh, how cute they are! Other roads do exist, of course, where the residents live and shop locally. However, the main road that runs through the town is where all the action is. We stayed two nights, shopped, and visited several restaurants. Our hotel balcony overlooked the magnificent mountains nearby.

Several restaurant owners confirmed that the "season" for them is the winter, although they do get a fair share of summer tourists and Greek people escaping the heat of larger cities for a relaxing, cool weekend. This is a very popular destination in the Parnassus Mountain range, hosting several ski lifts and chalets, small hotels, B and B's, etc. abound. And even those that don't ski love it here when the weather turns cold, sitting by the fireplace and watching the snowfall – a winter wonderland right in the middle of Greece!

To add to all this mountainous beauty, Arahova is not far away from beaches as we discovered when we looked at the map closely and chose our next destination.

Galaxidi

Leaving Arahova and driving past Delfi, we would go down through the mountains, into the rolling hills, and then the plains, leading us to the lovely coastal town of Galaxidi. We did not stop to visit Delphi, as we had already done that on a previous trip and well, basically, it was just too darn hot to walk around the ancient ruins and post a question or two to the Oracle! We waved as we drove by in our air-conditioned car.

We saw the cut-off for the town square – what we always look for first so we can orientate ourselves. We made the left turn, and then promptly, almost right on cue, we got lost! Just like practically every other place we visited, the twisting little roads led us 'round and 'round until we got to the shoreline and then asked directions to the hotel. We found it and settled in. We parked the car and decided to walk back down to the water because we did not want to have to go around the entire town again by car!

Walking just a bit down from our hotel, we found the strand… restaurants and small shops were lined up waiting for us. Admiring the natural beauty of this lovely cove, we took a long walk and then sat for dinner facing the beautiful sea and the bobbing boats. The perfect evening for a long day.

METEORA

Originally Published:

August 6, 2021

Many of the photos I have taken on this adventure do not do justice to the real thing. And here is where it is the truest of all: Meteora (Mehteh-ora).

This crowning glory of Central Greece is located in the Plain of Thessaly. These natural pillars and rock formations were formed 60 million years ago as the earth pushed through a lake. Natural elements formed the boulders over the years into what they look like today. This UNESCO World Heritage Site is a must-see for everyone!

Worth the Drive

We exit the main road coming up from Ioannina and begin a downward drive curving around a mountain. Each time we get to a straight road, we think we have arrived but no!… another climb up another mountain, through twisting roads where each bend takes up and around once more. This happens over and over again. It takes about forty-five minutes before we hit the main town at the base of Meteora. Beautiful scenery, true – but those roads are so narrow. We traveled slowly because you never knew what was coming around the corner. Whatever it might be, it may not be big enough for both of us to pass each other at the same time!

Kalambaka

Before you enter the town of Kalambaka, you see Meteora in the distance and as you get closer and closer, the towering formations look over the city, standing guard over it with its magnificent presence. This good-sized town offers great hotels, shops, and restaurants; three central squares form the Kentro (the center) and you have endless choices for a snack, a kaffe, or a meal. No matter where you go, where you sit, or where you walk, the rock formations are in full view and they are spellbinding. Photo ops galore! Just stop anywhere, and you are guaranteed a magnificent sight of the pillars and the monasteries built on top of them.

Monasteries

Of the original twenty-four monasteries existing in the sixteenth century to serve the Eastern Orthodox Church, only six are functioning today housing about fifty monks and nuns. Most of them are open to the public; we booked a tour to get up there and visit them.

You can certainly drive up there yourself and enter the monasteries that are open on any given day, but we wanted a tour to give us a break from driving and more importantly, to tell us more about the history of Meteora.

We visited three monasteries: the first required a climb of over 300 steps in various configurations to climb up and then climb down. I hesitated at first, but then figured, "When am I going to do this again?" I set out and did it! Naturally, it was slow moving for me – but people were kind and moved around me; some also offered help when I stopped to take a breather. Once up there, I was grateful that I made it – so much to see and absorb about monastic life both in ancient times and life for them today. The most fascinating site was the window with the pulley.

This was used until not so long ago to hoist up the monks and the packages brought back to the monastery. This prevented not only the enemy from coming up but any curious person as well. Looking down from this window, you see just how high up you are and realize that being hoisted up in a basket was not for the faint-hearted!

No Looking Back

Folklore, myth, or true story – nobody is really sure. Women were never allowed to climb the rocks and certainly not allowed in any of the monasteries. Back a few centuries ago, one of the major monasteries and its entire pillar caught on fire. Most of the men of Kalambaka were out in the surrounding fields, kilometers away; some were away from the town itself serving in the army or taking care of other necessities. The women began a water brigade, from the water source in the town all the way up the rocks and into the monastery. When the fire was put out, it was too late. Once they let them in, they could never not let them in again! One can never underestimate the power of women – then and now.

I've taken several photos here – they do not adequately reflect the majestic beauty of this area. You must see this place in person to experience the spectacular and striking views of Meteora!

Take out your bucket list and add this site right now!

CRETE

Originally Published:

August 20, 2021

Majestic. That is how I described Crete on our previous trip to this island, and it has remained true. Glorious mountains drop into the sea with waves pounding the shoreline against the rocks. Small towns are sprinkled through the hill tops built on several levels, creating a burst of color against the green foliage of the mountains.

We returned to Crete for one week because of our fond memories here based on beautiful vistas and delicious food. On that trip, we visited the ancient palace of King Minos of Knossos and envisioned life here when the ruins were intact. A path leading from the palace to the nearby town of Eraklion (now the capital city of Crete) still exists, and it was an awesome feeling to know that we stood on the same road as the inhabitants of the palace around 1600 B.C.

Actually, this was my third trip to Crete. I first visited over four decades ago with my aunt and other relatives. We stayed at a beach resort just outside Eraklion that was reached by a dirt round and stood out as there were no other buildings in sight. Zaf and I drove down there and found the resort which has now become a mega hotel among many other hotels all on the beach. Indeed, time has marched on.

Chania

This is pronounced HANIA (the c is silent)… a large city dating back to the Minion period and which became a Greek city-state in the Classical Greek period. Several ports – the Old Port is the largest and most visited – are situated around ancient Venetian and Ottoman ruins – and create a most stunning background to the waterfront restaurants and cafes… and of course, Old Town with its meandering alleys filled with shops and restaurants that are covered with the most beautiful bougainvillea. Long walks along the pier are a must for everyone and yet, ours is not very long. We prefer to sit at a café and watch the parade of people strolling by; we laugh at all the young people who walk by several times – all to catch the eye of a certain handsome young man or a pretty girl who is also walking by – so they can maybe walk together at some point. It's so lovely to watch them circling each other… ah, I remember those days!

Elafonisi

A long drive from Chania – about two hours but not straight! We climbed mountains and made hairpin turns that seemed endless; small towns met us at some of the curves. We were amazed at the number of hotels in each one; we also noted a good amount of stands selling natural honey, fruit, and moonshine! Along the way, suitcases were already being filled to the max – we made no effort to stop and buy.

We finally arrived at Elafonisi, and it did not disappoint. It has to be one of the most beautiful beaches anywhere. Parking was non-existent – all the spots were taken, some new spots were created (!), and some cars were parked along the beach road all the way to the top of the main road. We decided not to go down to the shoreline which we could see was already packed with swimmers and sun-tanners…. but as luck would have it, we found a delightful restaurant overlooking the entire beach and took our photos from there. With a full stomach, we braced ourselves for the return trip through the mountains back to the main road to our hotel.

The next thing we needed was a nap. So crawling into clean sheets in a nice cool room, I fell asleep to the rhythmic clip-clop of the horse-drawn buggies below as they made their way down the cobblestone streets just below our window.

Go Again

There is no way you can experience Crete in one week or two weeks; you really have to spend a good amount of time here to see every nook and cranny. It is Greece's largest island; you need to rent a car and go from one end of the island to the other – east to west – and then go north and south. Every corner on the road brings you to an unbelievably beautiful place. The love children of the 60's and 70's discovered the ancient caves here; Zorba danced here; The Minoan Palace is here; the Samaria Gorge is here; the endless cozy coves are here; the soaring mountains are here and the stretches of white and golden sand beaches that make you stand in awe are here. Time to pack your bags and get your tickets. This island is for you!

Retirement is fun! Every day joy comes from being at a happy place. We have our moments for sure, but we smile and know we made the right decision to...

Retire Well.

EVIA – KAVALA – THASSOS

Originally Published:

August 27, 2021

Evia

After an overnight ferry ride back from Crete, we drove about an hour and a half north of Athens to the island of Evia. We settled in our hotel outside of Eretria and planned our excursions. This included plenty of downtime relaxing around the pool and on the beach.

A pretty island with lots of curvy roads along the coast gave us views of sweeping beaches and coves on one side. On the other side were fields leading up to white homes tucked into green mountains. We stopped at a taverna on a cliff for lunch before we headed back to the hotel.

The beach town of Eretria was fun! It's a really small place with one street of shops along the water. There were so many seafood tavernas that offered delicious food and views of the clear blue sea. Looking for a hat was a delight – several shops had them, but I wandered into one at the suggestion of a man sitting in a small café. What a place! It was filled with beautiful home décor, clothes, shoes, bags, hats, jewelry, and anything you could imagine. The owner is a lovely woman with a great smile and personality. She spoke five languages! I tried on a couple of hats, but it wasn't until she pointed out one that I knew it was the right one! Truth be told, Zaf had seen it and told me to try it on, but I rejected it – and what a coincidence it was the one I bought!

She escorted us out to the street, where my eye caught the eye of the man who suggested I try that store; I smiled while pointing to the hat on my head. She said, "Ah, here is my husband!" He stood and said, "Welcome". They showed us the shop next door filled with absolutely stunning jewelry – I mean filled!!! One table after another showcased his personal designs in gold, silver, precious and semi-precious stones. All colors and gems gleamed throughout. I don't remember how long I was there, walking up and down the aisles, but it was a really long time. We bought a few items for ourselves and gifts. She then walked across the street with us and introduced us to the owner of the taverna to make sure we got the best fish in the place. Zaf chose it from a tank right there at the entrance!

We relaxed for a couple of days, then back over the bridge to Salonika, our home base. Here is where we re-group: laundry, car maintenance, emails, and computer calls to family and friends. Then, off to our next stop.

Kavala

A great harbor city dating back to the late 7th century B.C. It is the center of trade and tourism in the northern part of Greece as well as a major seaport. Roman and Ottoman empires ruled here throughout the centuries, and you can see remnants of their influence, especially in Old Town, which lies on the foothills of the great Byzantine Fortress. We climbed to the very top on a previous trip, so this time we admired it from afar. Dinner one night was at the very bottom of it facing the sea.

Built-in a U-shape, Kavala has a great walking strand where you can stretch your legs and enjoy the scenery. Little boats close in while larger ones sit further out. At one end, the ferry boats come in and out to drop off people and cars while picking up those who want to go to other islands. Our hotel was right there in the harbor so we saw the sun every morning as it shone across the bay of Kavala.

A bustling city with good restaurants and shops; there were people everywhere going and coming from work, eating out at night, and simply sitting at a café with friends. This was our third trip here because, well, we love it here!

Thassos

We drove from Kavala to Kithera, about thirty minutes away to take the ferry to Thassos. From the first glimpse, we noticed it was not like the other islands we visited. To begin with, it is very green with very tall mountains. From the port, there is only one road in and out. We took it and began the ride on the east side of the island, going south to the town of Limenaria. Just before we got to it, we pulled into our hotel.

Another pretty little beach town, where once again, we had fun! An entire street filled with stores and cafes. I spotted one incredible jewelry shop, but Zaf pulled me back! I guess he felt that enough is enough! We did walk through the long street a few times and stopped to eat at the numerous tavernas on the other side of the street along the sea.

Some stores had entrances from both the shopping side and the seaside so we used them often to go through. One such store was an arcade with a variety of games. One night, when there weren't any children around, we played table hockey to the amusement of the people passing by – my shrieks calling out to them, they laughed out loud. We had to return one more night, just for the sheer pleasure of being kids again. For those interested, we tied the first night and Zaf won the second night.

A drive around the bottom of the island and up on the west side of it was long, winding, and very green. You do not see the white-washed buildings dotting the coastline or in the mountains as much here. It is lusciously filled with foliage in various shades of light and dark greenery.

•

The most enjoyable part of exploring Greece is seeing the beauty up close. Zaf and I agree, that we have indeed... Retired Well.

MY TWO VILLAGES

Originally Published:

August 30, 2021

There was no way we would come to Greece and not go to the place where my parents were born and raised. To me, this is where I feel most connected to this land. So we packed up and hit the road.

In Central Greece, right in the middle of the mainland, is Lamia, the city where my sister and I were both born. You see it from the National Highway A1 that goes from Athens to Thessaloniki. Following the exit to the center of town, Zaf detoured into a side street that led out of town towards the town of Karpenisi. We visited Lamia once before. This is where he got lost for an hour, so it is not his favorite place. It doesn't bother me that he avoids it like the plague as there is not much to see there for tourists and exploring.

To make a note here: my parents met here in the restaurant my mother's uncle owned. Dad was a waiter, and my mom would come in to pick up the day's meal to take home. There are so many stories my mom told me about living here. You can read them in my memoir that I have started to save the history of our family (the sequel to this chapter of our lives, perhaps?). Hopefully, this will be my next retirement project.

We also drove through the outskirts of Karpenisi en route to the villages. We've been there a few times, and it boasts a lovely square in the middle of town. I remember one shop from 2005, above the square, where I sat in an internet café, drinking my frappe and sending emails. Now, of course, the internet is everywhere, including here in the mountains.

To get here is to begin the climb: a mountain road with twists and turns in and out of villages. With lanes so narrow, most cars come to a halt before they turn and inch forward to make sure that another car is not coming at them. We wondered how people live here, but I guess they have adjusted to the tightness of the spaces. It took about an hour and a half to get to this point from Lamia; we then began the real ascent into the forest. Our goal was to reach my mother's village, which is my heartbeat.

Small Village/Mikro Horio

You might think I am just describing the village, but I am not. That is the name of it: Small Village/ Mikro Horio. A picturesque square boasts a huge plane tree in the very middle surrounded by tables and chairs and two tavernas. Behind it, six faucets are drilled into the mountain, where clear water runs every day, all day. When you sit to order food, they bring you a pitcher and some glasses. You simply walk to the faucet and get your fill. Zaf drank right out of the faucet on several occasions by cupping his hands and slurping as much as he could!

Along the side of the square are steps that lead up to the homes that are built on the mountainside; my mother's being one of them. We climbed, we saw the house, and I wept.

Alas, I was only able to find one relative: my mother's second cousin Spiro. I did not have a phone number for him; I asked the hotel owner if he was in the village. He said he was, so I began to look for him after dinner where people gathered at the hotel terrace. And there he was! I wasn't 100% sure it was him, but I approached; he recognized my grandmother in my face. We embraced and pulled our chairs close together. We began to talk about our family tree; he promised to meet me the next morning to see what I had already put together. We did, and he was amazed at the extent of my knowledge of family genealogy. He introduced me to some other distant cousins and some of the villagers; they wanted to see my work. I unfolded the papers once again, and they were duly impressed. When Zaf showed up, he was surprised to see me sitting with about twelve people, most of them complete strangers – but that's me!

Big Village/Megalo Horio

The next day, we drove down the mountain, crossed the bridge, and then back to another mountain into my father's village. Once again, I kid you not, it is called Big Village/Megalo Horio. The two villages can see each other, and there is an undercurrent of competition of which one is prettier, has the best views, etc. I remember my parents talking about this very thing, with little dings at each other thrown in. To me, I love them both.

By asking a villager sitting under a tree in the main square, he pointed out my cousin's house. We knocked and there he was; his father and my father were first cousins. We met Niko in Athens on a previous trip, so this visit was shorter. Nevertheless, it was good to see him and share with him the family tree on my father's side. Then, a few short steps around the bend, brought us to my father's home. Now owned by someone else who cleaned it up beautifully, it still brought tears to my eyes to know that this is where dad walked every day of his life until he left for America in his late twenties.

Both of these villages, and several others, are folded into the mountains. Quaint and charming during the day, but in the late evening, when the lights come on, one at a time, across the entire slopes of massive trees, you are in awe of the beauty of the night. Over the years, this area has developed into a major skiing location in the winter and a perfect place for camping and hiking in the summer. The enormous trees, the valleys below, the sweet little villages, the sparkling brooks, and the gorges in between the mountains make this area a popular vacation spot all year long.

It is a bit of a drive to get here. As we left, I wondered if we would ever return. Although another trip to Greece is certainly doable, the ability to drive might not be, especially through the mountains with their precarious edges… we'll see. For now, I am grateful that I have seen my villages once again, and that to me is proof that we have… Retired Well.

KALAMATA

Originally Published:

September 13, 2021

Ever eat those delicious black olives in your Greek salad? This is where they come from. Those olives are called Kalamata Olives, so there you go!

A beautiful city, large and lively. Driving on the main road, we saw numerous, bustling stores, cafes, shops, restaurants, office buildings, etc. People were walking everywhere, and the traffic was just like any other modern city – snarly and endless. Just a few blocks away, the entire length of the city is hugged by a coastline perfect for swimming every day!

Kalamata has a large marina and port – very busy as it is the largest city in the Peloponnese after Patras. Several cultural events and sights are located here, famously the Maria Callas Alumni Association of the Music School of Kalamata and the Kalamata International Dance Festival. For those in the know, the Greek dance Kalamata originated in this city, too!

The beaches here are endless. You have a wide variety of places to go for a dip in the sea; most of them are in front of cafes/restaurants, so the tables and chairs, umbrellas, and beach cots belong to them. In some cases, you pay a nominal fee – but in most, you just order a soft drink or a meal and you are good to go! It's fun to watch service people maneuver around cars as they cross the street to get to the beach for their orders and then have to get back with their drinks and food!

We stayed at my cousin's place – where we stayed a few years ago as well – plenty of room and warmly received. We had great bonding time over three days. Elaine and I are first cousins; we both live in the USA but on different coasts! We spend our time together here lingering over breakfasts, taking short drives or walks mid-morning with a stop for lunch and some shopping, having a siesta each afternoon, and then dinner at the shore!

Messini

One morning, we drove to the site of the Ancient Messini about twelve kilometers outside the city. These are the ruins of the large, classical city-state of Messini This site has been excavated and partially restored.

It is open to the public, and we saw several people coming and going here. It has also been used for various cultural events held often in these parts of Kalamata. We stopped for lunch nearby overlooking the valley below and admiring the beauty of it all.

Antiquity

At the far end is the kastro, the fortress hosts a restaurant with an absolutely amazing view of the city below, a vast shoreline that spans the entire city from top to bottom on the western coast. The lights, the traffic, the people – a bundle of energy until the early hours of the morning!

The rocky hill fortress known as the kastro was home to its own Acropolis which was founded by a mythological figure called Faris. The city, then, was Farai… and this was mentioned by Homer in the Iliad, which comes as no surprise once you see the beauty of the kasto and Kalamata.

We just love visiting big cities like Kalamata after the seemingly endless drives up and down mountains and turning into every tiny lane to get to out-of-the-way little villages – it is such a positive statement that exploring Greece has given us a real insight not only into its geographical beauty but to its beautiful people as well.

MY GREEK COUSINS!

Originally Published:

September 20, 2021

Throughout our travels, we made some stops at places – basically, a night out, a drive-through, or a few days stay while we were waiting to fly home. These come to mind as I reflect on our journey throughout Greece. The best part of being there was the family members we visited with and sharing the experience.

Vouliagmeni

Just half an hour south of Athens, you come to this gorgeous seaside suburb known as the Athenian Riviera. Unbelievably beautiful hotels on the gorgeous shoreline, hovering over it on cliffs abound. A super long beach is "organized"… which means there are chairs and umbrellas already set up available for a fee instead of an empty beach where you need to bring your own. My cousin (mother's side) and her family flew into Greece the day before and settled here; we met up with them and had a delicious, long, leisurely dinner overlooking the sea!

Kifissia

This northern suburb of Athens is a beautiful place to live! Probably the most expensive area, but oh, the homes there are simply stunning. Large classical buildings with intricate and large balconies, surrounded by luscious gardens. The main avenue, Kifissia Avenue, is a mecca of shops and restaurants, offering the latest fashions and the most comfortable seats to enjoy a meal. My cousins (mother's side) live there, and it was such a joy to visit with them and catch up. The family tree I have put together was shared, and we all had a story to share and a name to add.

Nea Makri

With only one week left on our journey throughout Greece, we wanted to be close to the Athens Airport. We went to Athens several times already, and it was not something we wanted to do again, so we settled in at a beachfront hotel in Nea Makri, just about half an hour northeast of the airport. The feel of the hotel was tropical and beachy – looking out over the pool and the sea beyond was the perfect way to end our amazing trip. The shoreline is a good size and what is amazing is the number of tavernas and cafes that are lined up… we were there for six nights. It would have us another two weeks to visit each of them!

They all face the beautiful sea, so it was a real dilemma choosing where to eat each day. My cousin (father's side), who lives nearby in Pallini, drove up to join us, and we spent our time together talking about our family and viewing the family tree I put together; it was great that she was able to fill in some of the gaps I had about who everyone was and what branch they were on!

Marathon

Right next to Nea Makri is Marathon; we drove there, walked the strand on the beach, and enjoyed a tasty lunch. This city is known for two major events. The first was the battle of Marathon in 490 B.C. where the Athenians defeated the invading Persian army. The second is a legend – the runner Pheidippides, ran from here to Athens to announce the news of this victory. The length between the two cities is just over twenty-six miles, and this is the length of today's marathons starting from the 1896 Olympics in Athens when the first modern-day Olympics began. The Spirit of the Marathon statue is located in the park right in the central square of the town for all to see and admire.

We also met up with a newly found cousin (father's side) in a cute little café in Athens, spoke on the phone with another cousin (mother's side), and my mother's godson. All my Greek cousins rock!!!

Rafina

A town with a good-sized port – ferry boats take people to many of the islands. It is a great alternative to the port of Pireaus – which is huge and the traffic is considerable. We drove around and viewed the residential areas, saw the town square, and then went down the port where restaurants are lined up facing the harbor. We had lunch there and then drove down to the Athens airport – right across the street is a beautiful hotel where we spent our last night in Greece. With an early morning flight out, we were there in five minutes, checked in, and said goodbye to the land of our birth.

In looking at the map of Greece, we realized there was so much more to see that we just didn't have time for – and we were here for six months! This could only mean one thing – we must return to the land of the light: Greece!

With this in mind, we aim to Retire Well.

EVERYBODY LOVES GREEK FOOD!

Originally Published:

October 25, 2021

Greeks, like everything else they do, cook large. Each offering is sky high, and we soon saw that an order for two could easily feed four or more. Choices for appetizers are endless: meats, seafood, cheeses, dips, greens, etc. are available for lunch and/or dinner. You can explore different ones each day and along with your favorite aperitif (Ouzo!), it is the perfect way to begin your meal and get you going for the main event.

Then, you must have the famous Greek salad, which is served all over the world; none better than in the country where it was born! Greek salad is fresh tomatoes, cucumbers, onions, and peppers on the side topped with an extra-large piece of feta cheese, and sprinkled with village-grown oregano. Other types of salads are often on the menu and each, along with crispy, freshly baked bread, is a meal unto itself!

For your entrée, you can choose what the Greeks call "cooked plates" – every Greek claims that their mother's or their grandmother's Moussaka (Moosakah – with the accent on the kah!) is the best – and it probably is. Unfortunately, there is no way we can actually taste them all. What we did taste is a dish served all over Greece, and it has been unbelievably delicious everywhere we went – it is sometimes made with a bit of a twist – mountain people vs the islanders! Each one has been a masterpiece. It is our comfort dish… it warms the tummy, the heart, and the soul. We also tried the Pastisio (The Greek Lasagna), the stuffed peppers and tomatoes, the casseroles of string beans, onions, and/or other vegetables and greens, and the flavorful stews both with meat and without. Our favorite ones are the ones that come right out of the pot – just point to the one that you want – fresh and tasty that you can see and smell!

Vegetarian choices abound as they are the staple of the Mediterranean Diet - the best in the world! Spanakopita, (spinach pie) is a favorite in our family!

A large selection of meat dishes are offered. You can have skewers of lamb, beef, chicken, or pork. You can also have them served as lamb chops, lamb shanks, roasted lamb, chicken or pork chops, meatballs, or as pancetta, which are slices cooked to perfection and all are served with rice, roasted potatoes, and/or French fries.

What can I say about the seafood?! Literally, they are the catch of the day. In some places, you can see fish hanging outside the restaurant drying in the sun! Several times, the waiters took Zaf into the kitchen to pick his fish from a large tank. Trout, bass, salmon, tuna, sardines, squid, shrimp, lobster – all on the menu and served in a variety of ways – in salads, in tiny appetizer plates, as a main meal, with pasta, with rice or French fries.

After all of the above, there might not be room for dessert, but that did not stop us! Some of you might have already tasted the world-renowned Baklava and Kataifi, so you know how absolutely delicious they are. We also tried Melomakarina, Koulouriakia, and/or Galaktobourikia… and why not? Not one to miss out on any culinary experience, our daily selections were fun! Also in the mix, on some nights, we had ice cream. Sometimes we lingered at our table after dinner; sometimes we went to the ice cream store to buy a cone of our favorite or a dessert from the bakery next door, and then walked through the town square window-shopping and people watching.

The next chapter will cover the natural food grown and available to the local people, as well as where most restaurants buy their produce and fruits. This farm-to-table approach to the freshest food possible has been in existence from Ancient Greece until today. To whet your appetite even further, here are more photographs that speak for themselves!

The best way to explore a country is to eat the food! We did, and thus, we have Retired Well.

CROPS IN – LET'S EAT!

Originally Published:

November 1, 2021

On our recent retirement journey throughout Greece, we enjoyed delicious meals everywhere we visited. The freshness of the food did not surprise us. Farm-to-table is how the Greeks have eaten since the beginning of time. Many take their home-grown products to the open-air markets (the tomatoes are outstanding!), which take place in almost every city and town; some grow them for their own use.

Olive trees exist in the millions! Everywhere we went, we saw endless rows of them – they went on and on as far as you can see. In the plains of the Peloponnesus, home of the world-famous Kalamata olives found in Greek salads. In the fields and villages of Central Greece – and on the islands of the Aegean and Ionian Seas, the oldest tree is over 3000 years old. We went looking for it and found it on the island of Crete. It was amazing standing next to it knowing that our ancestors planted this tree for the generations to come; that includes us.

Right next to this ancient tree is a small tavern. We stopped for refreshments – the most hospitable people welcomed us. As we chatted, I spotted grapes hanging right above us on the trellis! In Nea Makri, an enterprising man brought his grapes to market in a very low-cost way. Simply delicious!

We loved wandering around the marketplace picking up small souvenirs and what-nots. We watched as fruits and vegetables were brought in and laid out for our selection. Tomatoes, eggplant, squash, etc. It was good to know the ones we were served at the tavernas came right from the farm!

Fish was incredibly fresh; it was a common sight to see them hanging out to dry. Allowing us to pick a fish from a tank was my favorite thing for Zaf to do! Knowing that our appetizer was today's catch added to our enjoyment. The food stalls in the marketplace in Thessaloniki showcased the freshest fish you can buy and relish for dinner that night. A bit of grilled seafood with lemon and oil on it, and we were good to go!

The local people were not the only ones enjoying fresh meat from the marketplace. The butcher shops also got to buy their selections and make it possible for people to take them home and cook up any way they wanted. Some restaurants have a unique way of showing what is available on their menu!

Let's get some Greek Food! People we met in our travels and our own backyard have told us that it is a typical answer to "What are we going to eat tonight?!" Zaf and I were raised with Greek food on the table daily; the tastes and smells were incredible, and we thought that everyone ate the way we did. Our school lunches were feta cheese and tomato sandwiches, maybe a dolmade or two on the side, and a kourambhie (butter cookie) for dessert. At the time, we were embarrassed sitting next to the other kids eating peanut butter sandwiches. Over time, while we continued to enjoy our cuisine, Greek food in the world caught on and it is highly-touted to be the best way to eat for healthy living.

I remember someone asking me if we (Greeks in America) celebrated Thanksgiving – which I thought was a weird question. My response was, "Of course we do, we have turkey and yams, cranberry sauce, and corn – but we also have spanakopita, Greek salad, and feta cheese. Dessert was pumpkin pie and baklava!"

How wonderful that people have discovered scrumptious Greek food. Knowing that others eat as we do brings us joy and contentment.

And thus, we have Retired Well.

THE BEAUTIFUL TAVERNAS OF GREECE

Originally Published:

November 12, 2021

Tavernas and Kafeneeos are the center of Greek life. They are embedded in Greek culture and history.

This is where people meet for a quick cup of kafe or to linger over a meal. No matter how small a village is, there is always a taverna or two. They date back to ancient times when men would sit and philosophize about life, politics, weather, and the like. In many places, especially in rural areas, rooms are attached for those who don't want to venture far from the village square.

When we arrived in Athens, we were eager to have Greek food… alas, the city was in lockdown and the only thing we could do was get it delivered. If we ventured out, it was take-away. Delicious nevertheless, but the menu options were limited.

Outdoor Dining

When the country opened, tavernas and restaurants were allowed outdoor dining. Everyone made a mad dash to them, including us! It was like a switch was turned on and everyone could now see the light… the beautiful Grecian light created by the sea and sky.

Some of my favorite places are along the shoreline where tavernas are lined up in a row. Staff members stand outside next to the menu board and call out their special of the day; they invite you in to taste their fare. They size you up and try to determine where you are from and in what language you speak. They try English, French, Italian, German, etc. Amazingly, they converse enough to bring you in, seat you, and then take your order in many different tongues!

Thatched Tops

Each taverna and café has a place on the beach under a thatched or wooden top, with colorful tablecloths and napkins, various style chairs, and interesting décor. Some tables were set up right on the sand, just a few feet away from the water. The most popular color choice is blue, of course. Perhaps representing the glorious sky and celebrated seas of Greece. You can't help but notice how often blue chairs are used; to us, they represent the best in Greek dining. These are the ones we picked most often – a throwback to the memories we have from visiting Greece in our youth.

As the weather gets warmer, bathers set up their towels on the sand, leave their bags at their table, order an enormous number of appetizers and aperitifs which they nibble on throughout the day, and spend the day swimming and eating.

Many stayed into the evening having yet another meal.

Dining Late

New arrivals appeared right around 8:00pm, and the tables filled up quickly. Greeks, like most Europeans, eat late. They stay until midnight and on the weekends until 1 or 2am. You can always tell who the tourists are – they show up at 6:00pm and are done by 7:30! Sad to say, we were part of this group, although as the summer progressed, we too started eating later and later. We met such interesting people from all over the world at these tavernas, both the diners and the dining staff!

In addition to the delectable food, the key to eating out in Greece is that you can sit at your table as long as you want – nobody bothers you to hurry along so they can seat other people. Greeks do not just eat – they dine. They also order food in layers – appetizers, then salad, then the main meal, then fruit, then dessert. It takes hours! They linger and this is the custom. Unless you flag down the staff, they do not present the check. This is true for lunch and dinner. Kafe drinkers are notorious for buying a single cup at 3:00pm and staying until 8:00pm!

Taverna Views

The views from many of these tavernas are stunning. They include the sea, a lake or river, bridges, and mountains; they are set on sidewalks, beach fronts, village squares, and rooftops. As we traveled around, we discovered the most charming little tavernas in coves, tiny hamlets, and on the side of the road. The most modest of décor was often simply the best!

Taverna Names

The names of these places made sense and, in some cases, made us laugh. Greek gods are natural; we saw Poseidon and Neptune all over Greece, and they were typically seafood places. Aphrodite, Zeus, Apollo – they were all there. Zorbas was another one we encountered in numerous towns. But quite often, we saw Platanos (which is a large plane tree) on the beach with no foliage in sight! Or Meltemi which is the warm wind where towns where the heat pounds on you daily with no breezes or sign of relief.

There are numerous modern kafeneeos with high stools and tables that the younger people enjoy sitting at daily. Very crowded at certain times of the day and very loud, both in conversation and music. We avoided those. We prefer tiny places with six or eight tables, grandma in the kitchen, the grandson bussing tables – you know which ones I mean: the family-owned restaurants that span generations. Nothing beats food that has passed the test of time.

Natural Beauty

The absolute best part? The twinkle lights that are turned on above the tables when the sun has set, but that in no way compare, to all the brilliant stars in the night sky above. Being able to see this natural beauty every night for six months, we know, for sure, that we have Retired Well.

THE ENDURANCE OF THE GREEKS

Originally Published:

November 29, 2021

The strength of any country is its people. The ability and stamina to carry on is inherent in the Greeks. Evident in their struggles to overthrow invading armies, occupation of foreign powers, wars, economic turndowns, and day-to-day living that is simply called life.

The Elder

I have developed an enormous interest in the older generation. Perhaps it is because I am now semi-retired and that classifies me as being "elderly". One of the most fun conversations I had with my cousin Maria in Greece when we were reminiscing about my past trips there was about the evolution of being called **Miss** to being called **Madam**! These two words are an expression of respect, I know, but it hit me hard! And this was thirty years ago! Maybe it was because I was with my niece who resembles me, so it might have been natural to assume that she was the younger and I was, well... **the elder!**

In touring through Greece, it became very apparent that the older folks were out and about. Their actions spoke loudly. On city streets and country roads; going to the market and walking back with their little bag of groceries or pulling along their carts. To and from church, certainly. Often, they were lined up outside a store or a bank patiently waiting for the doors to open. They get their hair and nails done. They walk their dogs. They held cell phones, and it was quite charming hearing them yell into it as though it required a stronger, louder voice than just speaking into it like a landline phone. Some had canes they used to help them walk and some held them as props. As I was coming out of the pool one day, an eighty-year-old was slowly coming down the pool steps and holding on to the banister; I stood by just in case she slipped... she said, "I've got to watch where I am going these days, as I don't move as fast." I smiled and said, "Me too!" She got in with her little hat and began her swim as though she was a mere youngster.

Throughout the day, from early morning until late in the evening, they could be found at the local kafeneeo, especially the men. Time and time again, around five p.m. a group of women, all freshly dressed up, would gather at the kafeneion and spend their evening enjoying little snacks and their kafe. Some were even seen smoking! They animatedly chatted and laughed, often calling out to a nearby table, filled with yet another group of ladies.

Those that didn't go out were seen sitting on their balconies talking with their neighbors who sat on their balconies as pastries were passed back and forth.

The really old are modestly dressed in dark colors; the not-so-old wear modern clothes with a good smattering of pants and tops, which in my mothers' day was unheard of! Even when I visited here as a young woman, back in the 1970s, older women wearing pants was just not done. Hair is neatly combed, and many sported the "just came from the salon" look. One night, while having dinner with our friends, Lambro and Maria, a woman about 65 years old walked by with her family. She had on a nicely cut dress with large swirling black and white flowers on it, a white sweater over her shoulders, pearls around her neck, black low-heeled shoes, and a black patent leather purse. I nearly burst out crying; that is just what my mother wore, along with my aunties, when "going out" for the evening. The classic look never gets old.

For many, work has not stopped… not sure if it is a needed income issue or if they do it to keep themselves busy: the guy with the big white apron that is hawking the fresh fish caught that day; the lady selling embroidery and linen tablecloths at the open air market; the man picking up empty cups and trash and then combing the sand at 7:00am so the visitors are welcomed to a clean beach. We saw them driving tractors and motorbikes (yikes!); many greeted us as we sat down to a meal and then served us dish after dish; my cousin Spiro is 86 years old – he is in excellent shape, smart as a whip, works the cell phone like a twelve-year-old, drives and does some traveling, and also takes care of his wife who is not that agile. As we enjoyed our meal one day, we were serenaded by a man who played the accordion and sang our favorite Greek songs.

We saw quite a number of these elderly people working the fields. Bent over from the waist, they lifted and pulled all sorts of crops and loaded up bags or small trucks. Some were hoeing, some were planting. You wanted to shout out to them to stop – that someone younger should be doing this hard labor, but innately they know that if they stopped, they would simply fade out of life. For this IS their life – it is what keeps them going – it is what they know. I salute them all.

What is their secret? How they eat for sure. It has been said that Greece has one of the best diets in the world, if not THE best. A large amount of seafood is consumed; natural greens and other vegetables appear at every table; feta cheese (my personal favorite) along with fresh fruits are eaten daily. The island Ikaria has been touted "as where people forget to die" – they live into their 100s in good shape and with sharp minds.

Walking everywhere has sustained them. It is simply a fact of life established early on when they were children where transportation was sporadic at best. My mother often repeated the story of how she went into labor and began the long walk to the clinic. How, along the way, an army jeep pulled alongside and swept her up to take her there.

I like the fact they are so independent. They just do what must be done. Perhaps they might have a relative, neighbor, or friend who can do their errands or drive them. But why? They get up, washed, and get dressed to tend to the business at hand.

Observing them is an inspiration. For sure, when I grow up, I want to be just like them! Aiming for that goal, it is necessary for me and Zaf to Retire Well.

THESSALONIKI

Originally Published:

December 17, 2021

A five-hour drive north of Athens is the city of Thessaloniki. We purposefully set out on a Sunday morning for our first trip (we visited ten times!) there this past summer, when traffic is typically minimal. Coupled with the lockdown restrictions for citizens who are not permitted to go from one province to another, the road was practically empty. With two pit stops along the way, we arrived in the late afternoon.

Zaf often boasts that, although born in a neighboring small village, he attended second and third grade in Thessaloniki, Greece's second largest city. With over one million people living here today, Zaf takes great pride in this city's historical importance as the crossroads of many cultures, religions, and industries.

Built by the ancient Greeks, this city goes back to 315 B.C., named after the half-sister of Alexander the Great; it means Victory of the Thessalians. It was to honor the victory over the Phocians, led by Philip II of Macedon. It would be well worth it to spend some time here, especially if you love history. Numerous sections of walls and arches are scattered throughout the city as remembrances of the big wall that once surrounded the city in ancient times as fortifications against invading armies. Additionally, interspersed by glorious cathedrals and tiny churches dating back hundreds of years, modern buildings host offices and shops; wide open plazas are surrounded by restaurants and cafes, as is the glorious shoreline and the crowning glory, the White Tower which was part of the ancient wall and served as a watchtower. You can visit the tower and climb the winding steps to the very top… the view will dazzle you!

Take the time and make the effort to drive up the sloping streets to the upper areas of this city – or you can take a tour bus. The view of the bay is spectacular as are the winding streets and architecture of the older homes and buildings. This city has numerous squares – large and small scattered about in all neighborhoods. The biggest and most known is Aristotelous Square… shops and cafes abound. It is the best place to be seen and to meet up with family and friends. One area that we love is called Panorama, with beautiful stately homes, buildings, churches, and restaurants overseeing the entire city and the sea beyond. Another favorite area is the Ladadika district. Originally, it was a prominent center of olive oil presses, which is how it got its name: ladi is the word for olive oil. It then transitioned into a red-light district.

By the 1980s, it gentrified into a bustling dining area with restaurants, kafeneeos, clubs, etc. The winding, narrow, cobblestone streets charm and delight you as you walk around amid the preserved 19th-century buildings. We have never visited Thessaloniki without stopping there for a long, lingering, lunch.

Thessalonik is a mixture of the old and new, and it all works together to create a sophisticated atmosphere of the present without forgetting its remarkable past. Greeks affectionately call it Saloniki, but to the outside world, it is known as Salonika.

We drove there one day, just twenty minutes from where we were staying. An amazing number of cars and trucks zoom in and out of lanes, zigzagging to get in front of you so they can move faster. An interesting thing to see in this city is the parking spots – there are none!

Double parking abounds – the lanes, although wide enough, get smaller and smaller. Nobody seems to mind though; it is a way of life here. We chose to park in a garage after we drove around for about fifteen minutes, looking for a space, all to no avail. On subsequent trips into the city, when the lockdown was removed, we discovered a ferry service taking us from near our hotel to the port of Salonika; being such a walkable city, we opted to eliminate the drive and its traffic/parking issue and simply sail into town.

The first couple of times we visited there, during the lockdown, we were astounded to see so many cars and trucks on the road; once inside the city, the number of people out and about was incredible. Not all stores were open, of course; restaurants were closed, but many had a window/door open for take-away. An endless number of people were standing outside or sitting on benches sipping coffee and munching away. Masks were worn, but we wondered: "This is what lockdown looks like here?"

The hotel staff faithfully prepared our "daily" exit papers before we left the lobby. Not once were we asked to present them. The desk clerk told us that she, as a citizen, could not leave the area due to the lockdown; I asked her, "Since no one is checking paperwork, how would anyone know if it was you or us, the tourists?" She was surprised to hear that Salonika was packed with people walking around or sitting by the sea enjoying the sunshine and the view.

Another of our favorite places is the old marketplace. Some souvenir shops and stores were closed, but the produce, meat, seafood, dry goods, and grocery stalls were all open, and they were a sight to see! Vendors stand out in front and shout out the prices of the day – emphasizing the amazing discounts they are offering which beat out the competition! "Hurry in! Prices are only good for today!" The smells and sounds invoke the ancient "agora" dating back thousands of years.

We found a fabulous hotel, just outside Zaf's childhood village, Kerasia. We could not find it easily though. As the area has changed with new buildings and other structures, and with old landmarks shut down, we drove around a little bit. Then, with bad directions from a woman who insisted that the hotel was through some narrow roads and then off to the right by the beach, we got lost. A kind man called the hotel for us (we didn't have our Greek phone set up yet) and got the correct directions. The hotel was absolutely beautiful, but nowhere near the beach!

The next day, we toured all the villages in the area and found Zaf's memories... some places still exist, and others have disappeared forever. No matter. Wherever you go in these areas, you have a view of the magnificent Thermaic Gulf of Salonika. Peeking through the clouds early in the morning, you see only the mountains, but when they float away, the entire city comes into view with its full impact of how big it is and how lovely it sits, nestling into the hills, with its white buildings and blue sea as a neighbor.

The highlight of our stay here was finding Zaf's lifelong friend, Lambro. He and his wife, Maria, greeted us with much exclaim and many hugs (yes, indeed!). We sat on their veranda, and they reminisced about their childhood together, remembering how, as boys of eight and nine, they played soccer together on a dirt road that today is the main street running through the village where the shops and restaurants are. He was excited to discover through social media on his phone he could talk to us more often. It is sad to say, but he passed away just a few months after our trip there... RIP Lambro.

We made Saloniki our mainstay. We returned to this hotel/area ten times during our six-month stay. They took excellent care of us; they kept the same large and comfortable room ready for us; they had a great laundry service, a gorgeous pool, delectable food, and an amazing staff! It was our home away from home.

If we had to pick a place to live in Greece, Saloniki would be it! We know this would be a great place to Retire Well.

HALF A YEAR IN GREECE

Originally Published:

January 3, 2022

▬▬▬

OUR SIX-MONTH RETIREMENT JOURNEY IN THE LAND OF OUR BIRTH: GREECE

We fully expected everyone's reaction to our plans to sell everything and live out of our suitcases for six months would be: ARE YOU NUTS?!!! Some people did say this very thing, and some, more politely, hesitated for about three seconds and then blurted out, "Are you sure about this?" Yup, we were. Most of my family and friends have always known that I was gutsy and bold. Zaf certainly learned I was so soon after we met… but to radically change the way we live was really large, even for me!

Most people who heard about our plans to live in Greece were very happy for us. They wished us well and thought we were very brave! The lady who processed my international driver's license was beside herself with such happiness when she heard of our plans. My primary doctor, skin doctor, and neuropathy doctor (full check-up before we left!) were each extremely supportive and joyful. Neighbors, clients, friends of clients (!), and even the hosts of our temporary housing before we left were thrilled to hear about our plans.

I have retired. To be more precise, I have semi-retired as the work ethic instilled in me by my immigrant roots was not allowing me to come to a complete stop… and the thought of not having anything to do decided me to stay active as long as possible. My husband, Zaf, retired twice within the last five years, but each time went back to part-time work because, well, he was bored. He officially retired for good about two weeks before our trip to Greece.

Birthplace

Three years ago, we decided to visit our birthplace – Greece – for a length of time while we were still young enough to travel around and see the places we never saw on prior trips there. Perhaps it can be thought of as brave, but we thought of it as returning to our original home to re-root ourselves… a dream we've had for several years as we worked hard towards retirement and what would it look like.

I was born in Lamia, Greece, and came to the USA when I was nine months old. Growing up in New York City in a predominantly Greek neighborhood, the first ten years or so were spent in a cultural cocoon. Neighbors were mostly Greek, the lady at the bank, and the grocer as well. A private Greek school attached to a Greek Orthodox Church was the center of my world. It wasn't until I was old enough to venture out a little bit that I realized there was a whole other world out there!

Zaf was born in Nea Mehaniona and grew up in Kerasia, a suburb of Thessaloniki. He arrived in New York when he was ten years old. Growing up in New Jersey and Massachusetts, his community was also primarily Greek. He learned English mostly by playing soccer with the neighborhood boys before he was able to catch up with the school grade he belonged in. High school was his entry into the larger world where he made friends and excelled in sports and schoolwork. His name is Zafiris but was shortened to Zaf to make it easier to pronounce for those who didn't speak Greek!

Embracing this new adventure was daunting, and yet, we were never afraid of following through with our plans. We got our tickets, our Greek passports, and our international driver's licenses; we rented a car for the entire length of our stay, and we notified relatives and friends that we would soon be there. Being in the throes of the worldwide pandemic, we got both vaccinations and got tested before we left. We waited for our departure date with much patience on most days; on others, we talked ourselves silly about what we would do and what we would see once we got there.

Agreement

We had discussed what each of us envisioned for this trip and were happy to discover that we shared the same vision, desire, and guts to take this retirement kickoff journey. We explored lots of options: Retire and go right away. Retire and wait? Rent out the house or sell the house? How long would we be traveling? Where would we live when we come back? The pandemic was in full force – the world was changing… what would happen to us if we were stranded there? Not a bad place to be stranded in – but you know what I mean! Lots and lots of research took place – mostly by me… once I had the details/options, we discussed them and made our decisions.

Got Rid Of The Old

The first step towards our journey: We sold the house and cars; we got rid of "jobs" although we kept one business that we shared, and I kept my online business. We got rid of tons and tons of stuff: furniture, clothes, and a garage full of odds and ends. Opting out of the gazillion e-mails we get daily, putting all our remaining bills on autopay, hiring a manager for our business, etc. ensued. I was also happy to learn many things can be done online, so I tucked away my passwords into my wallet and planned to follow up on any lingering items I could not get to before we left.

Three Grew Into Six

The only thing that changed was the length of our journey. We had originally planned on three months, but when the manager of our new housing development told us it would take six months to build our new home, Zaf and I immediately looked at each other and grinned: six months in Greece!

Something New

We decided where we would live once we returned. A 55+ development beckoned – we put down our deposit, picked out the "plan," chose all the tiles and cabinets and such, and signed all the paperwork. The staff there assured us that any follow-up required could be done online. Whew!

Spending an afternoon looking at cars narrowed down our choices, so we had an idea of what we would be buying when we got back.

Our furniture was stored with automatic monthly payments set up. Global bank transfers were identified, and the app was added to my cell phone, so we would get the funds to spend once abroad.

Temporary

Our house sold faster than we thought, so we packed two additional suitcases and moved into temporary housing for two and a half months. At first, it felt really weird living somewhere else, but I soon realized – and shared my thoughts with Zaf – that this is how we will be living for months and months; we might as well get used to it. He agreed, and we settled in.

Are We Lucky Or Not?

It's surreal on most days this was all happening; it felt very strange. Once or twice, I had a fleeting thought – are we crazy people?! I asked myself, "How many other people would do this…at our age?" Did I worry about the future? No. And yes. What would happen if one of us got sick or hurt? What would happen if we hated living on the road? What would happen if the world got more chaotic and we had to stay longer than we planned?

Believing that faith and courage would see us through brought me peace when I thought of these things. Knowing that Greeks live and love large sustained me, leaving no doubt that we would be received with open arms.

We had planted the seeds and embarked on the reaping of what we had sowed. What will be, will be, as there would be no turning back. And so – perhaps to see a wizard or two – but definitely to see the magnificent ruins and white, sandy beaches of Greece, the lushness of Tuscany, the Mediterranean Sea – to meet interesting new people and see new places, find adventure, and do fun things awaited us. The Art of Exploring, indeed.

Six months is not a long time after all… it went by in a flash. We returned safely and began settling in at our new home. Memories are still strong and yet, the future beckons us to do more traveling and exploring. Not bad for a pair of Retire-Agers™.

I THINK IT WOULD BE BETTER OVER THERE

Originally Published:

January 21, 2022

We moved into our new home in September and spent a couple of weeks opening boxes that were placed all over the house. Keeping track of the box cutter was a chore! It was, nine out of ten times, forgotten under the endless wrapping paper; a couple of times, we thought it was thrown away as we bagged it all up. I can't begin to tell you how high the empty boxes were – they were a bigger mess when flat than when they were full. You must break them down and then cut them so they fit the garbage can... the good news is it was Zaf's job to do this. I, on the other hand, began the washing.

Washing everything wrapped in newspaper went on and on and on... and since the appliances were all new, we had to learn how to use the dishwasher. I had to stop washing at one point because the clean stuff were piling up, and I hadn't decided where everything was going to go yet. Zaf suggested that we make a first stab, and then we would rearrange it all later. I continued non-stop for a few days and put them in the cabinets I thought would work. We have moved things around several times based on how we use them.

Speaking of appliances... EVERY single one of them is "smart;" this is a technological term that means it has lots of bells and whistles I can access online and with an app on my phone... I think. The guy came out to show us how to use them with the technology, and it was truly amazing to see how it all works. To date, we haven't used them once. We just use the On or Off knobs. They are all SMARTER than us!

Priority was setting up the bed and getting the toiletries in place. We had set up a bin as our starter box, so we hunted around for it, found it, and got the job done. We ate out for a few days and then went food shopping. We set up the coffee maker on the counter, over to one side, near the refrigerator. Then, we had to make sure that all the coffee things – mugs, sugar, cream – were in the cabinet immediately above. I bought a holder for the K-cups, but it didn't fit on the counter or the cabinet above; it did fit the cabinet below. This was one of our first priorities, because, hey, you gotta have a cup of coffee in the morning!

And then, one day, while I was doing the laundry, I heard a big bang. I ran to the laundry area and see water all over the floor. The machine had stopped… it exploded all over the place. Mopping was not on the chore list for the day but mopping I did. I tried to restart the machine but to no avail. Zaf came home from running errands, and we decided to buy a new one; we also did a "we might as well" thing too - buy a new dryer as well. More bother and more expense… not to mention we paid to store these two big items along with the rest of our stuff. You tell me: were we idiots or not? We knew both were pretty old, but for some reason thought they would still have some life in them. Just like us!

We had arranged for a closet organizer company to create our closet space, so our clothes and shoes remained in the clothes moving boxes which we opened on the living room floor; we dressed out of them for about a week. That was fun, especially when I had to put my entire body's upper half into the box to find my shoes! Ironing was not going to happen, so pull-on pants and a top I ironed by running my hands over them were the uniform of each day. Finally, the closet was done, and we spent an entire day hanging everything up and arranging shoes… so easy to use and nice to look at now!

We did have differences of opinion (ahem!), of course. In our old house, our pantry was a cupboard with overflow in the garage. Here, we have a large, on the entire wall, double-door pantry with a top and bottom. Pull-out drawers are worth every penny we paid for them. Zaf unloaded all the cans and bottles of the beverages we drink; some went into the fridge and the rest were stored in the pantry. That is perfectly fine except for the fact they were placed on the FIRST SHELF OF THE BOTTOM PANTRY… RIGHT WHERE I LOOK AT EVERY DAY WHILE SEARCHING FOR THE SALT! I waited a few days (ahem!) before I broached the subject that perhaps it might be better if we put the things we use EVERY DAY on this shelf and the other things on the lower shelves since we don't use them EVERY DAY! We compromised, and he moved them to the top pantry which is mostly storage of kitchen things.

As we unwrapped the items, we scratched our heads and exclaimed, "WE KEPT THIS?" When we couldn't find something we thought we packed, we wondered, "DID WE THROW IT OUT? What were we thinking???" The bad news is we ended up with a few things we should not have kept, and the good news is finding the familiar items that made our last house a home, and now with a new purpose, it would do the same here.

We spend days deciding on the décor. The question of, "Does this go here or there?" loomed above us. A vase was placed on the credenza and then moved to the bookcase. A chair that would not be kept was put into use because I would not have a place to sit while watching TV until the new chair arrived. We had to wait for over a month to get a couch, so nothing else could be "situated" until it arrived (size and color had to be considered). Pictures were placed on the floor against the wall where they would be hung until I changed my mind and moved them around and around. A rug I ordered was too big; scrounging around the garage I found a marvelous runner Zaf's mother made back in Greece many years ago; cleaned and brushed, it now lives under the table in our entry hall.

I'm still at it – I look at something and say, "I think it would be better over there". Zaf sighs and heads for the garage to get the hammer, nails, and other mystery tools he may need. The one thing we agreed upon right from the start was where the big TV in the living room would be placed…only because it was the only wall available – the other two walls have windows, and the fourth "wall" opens into the kitchen.

So here we are… our new home has taken shape. The one thing I miss though is color. In the old house, the walls were deep red, dark green, light green, etc. Here, it is all white and grayish. I'm putting up lots of pictures to bring color into the rooms, and it is working... somewhat. I am in withdrawal about this, but other than that, we have Retired Well.

RETIREMENT – WHAT'S IT ALL ABOUT?

Originally Published:

May 9, 2022

There are a lot of retirement groups on social media that I follow. A large number of posts are made daily in each group; each makes its own statement about what is on their mind. All are part of the retirement community, and I believe each group's goal is to increase the number of people in the group. More importantly, they desire to have these people engage in conversation, like, follow, etc.

The posts vary and depending on the skills of the writer, they are interesting in their own way. Mostly, they are inspiring and uplifting with adages, quotes, and prayers. Some simply say, "Have a Beautiful Day" or "Happy Birthday!" A lot share their travel photos with a recap of where they visited… or about a trip to a local wine vineyard, cultural festival, beach, etc. Many write about illnesses and financial and/or family crises; they give explicit details and ask for our prayers and support.

A selected few are looking to make friends to chat with and perhaps visit in person if they live close by. I've also seen posts where they want to meet a "significant other." Those are frowned upon and even removed from the platform. I suspect they go ahead and send private messages to each other. Just like online dating, you've got to be wary (although Zaf and I met online – but that is another story!). I realize people get lonely and use social media to express themselves and to feel connected to other people; this is how they reach out to the world.

I try to respond (not for meetups!) or at least give them a "like," but sometimes I am just not in the mood. When I see forty-seven posts telling me to have a good day, I try not to roll my eyes. When fifteen people are asking for retirement financial advice about how to invest, what can I say? I'm no expert. When people are looking for solutions to medical issues, why ask us?

They should be having a chat with their doctor – suppose what other people are saying makes them sicker? When I see thirty-five people sharing their drama, I scroll down. Is this fair? No, it is not. I offer no excuses. What I truly am against, are those who respond with negative comments or say to those that are sad and depressed to "get on with it." Why hurt people with insensitive remarks?

Recently, some people reacted to a post I made about filling our calendar with things to do. By far, the responses were positive. For example, people said, "Do it now…why wait?" or "Fill up every moment and enjoy!" However, one person said, "You don't have to be busy all the time…relax" and another said, "Retirement is about taking it easy." I paraphrase, but you get my meaning. Relaxing is definitely part of our daily "tasks." I take a nap every afternoon! Zaf sits in his lounger and watches sports for about an hour before dinner time.

Often, he dozes off, but he never owns up to that!

One person admonished me for traveling and being active because of pandemic restrictions. Really? Airplanes, hotels, and tourist destinations are filled with people. Shops, restaurants, schools, etc. are open with no mandates. Where is this person living? I responded kindly, reminding her to be open to the fact that the world keeps on spinning… even though I do recognize that the virus is still out there; we need to be mindful of it. Plus, booking hotels and travel accommodations can be exhausting.

My favorite posts are the jokes and funny things people send in. Some are a bit risqué; some are about politics; some are about daily life with family members or friends, and some are just photos that make you look twice. I share them with Zaf, and we laugh out loud. Sometimes I re-post them on my own feed so others can enjoy it.

Zaf and I are still planning to explore. As long as we can… and this is pointed at you too… we plan to be active. I already see signs that we are slowing down – we get tired doing simple things such as gardening or laundry – things that were easier to do a few years ago. But that is not keeping us from doing the things we love to do.

Retirement is about relaxing, for sure. Mornings are not a dash out of the house; a long stretch of an afternoon happens every day; evenings are not filled with chores because there wasn't time to do them during the day. The pleasure comes from knowing I don't have to do a darn thing if I don't want to… and doing every darn thing I want to do. It also gives you the time to pick up new hobbies that are great for both your physical and mental well-being. For example, taking a yoga class online is great for your physical health and allows you to pause to relax. We have been conditioned to be go-go-go for years, and you may notice it takes you some time to adjust.

The ancient Greeks said, "In all things moderation;" I emulate my ancestors. How much relaxing do I need to do? Spending my days sitting in a chair watching TV or reading has its limits. Eventually, you have to rejoin the world. We relax on the beach when we are in Hawaii; we relax by the pool when we are on a cruise. There you go, activity and relaxation…. now that is a good combo!

So, my answer to retirement – What's it all about? It's whatever you want it to be! Borrowing from a teenager's popular response to everything in their life, I use it frequently. Do you want to meet up for coffee on Monday or Tuesday? Whatever. Can you lead the book club discussion group next month? Whatever. Should we go to Hawaii in September or October? Whatever.

EXPLORING THE PANAMA CANAL

Originally Published:

June 10, 2022

We learned about the Panama Canal back in our school days, and along with the significance of establishing a new trade route, I always thought it was an exotic place to visit. It did not disappoint when we took off for a fifteen-day cruise and saw firsthand what it looked like and how it functions. Retirement is looking better and better every day!

One of the requirements, of course, was to have a negative COVID test. We took the test two days before we left. Zaf got his results the very next day; I did not. I kept calling and the automatic response was that it was pending. Pending and pending, all through the day and up to 11:00pm the night before our departure. A fitful sleep and an early morning rise to call again – still pending. What to do! We left for San Pedro, the port of Los Angeles anyway with knots in our tummies. Checking in brought me to a station they set up for testing – courteous enough not to charge me as I had proof that I did the testing. I spent about fifteen minutes with a lot of apprehensions – thoughts running through my head about not being able to board and returning home ran rapidly; I got the negative, embarked, and breathed easier!!!

Unpacking once is a key feature of cruising! Getting familiar with the ship came next as we explored and noted the key places of the ship: restaurants, pool, and the casino! At our first night dinner, we sat with another couple; we shared cruise experiences and getting-to-know-you type of questions – "Where are you from? Where are you cruising next?"

After two days at sea, we reached Puerto Vallarta; we had been there before on a prior cruise, but we took the shore excursion anyway to see and learn new things and to get off the ship! Another day at sea and then Huatulco, Mexico; we took the shore land/sea excursion which we liked very much. This is a beautiful place, and we decided it would certainly be a place to return and explore its beautiful beaches, cute town square, and first-rate hotels.

We spent the next two days at sea, sunning by the pool, reading, and napping while Zaf played pickleball on the top deck.

Costa Rica was our next stop; again, we had been there before, but shore excursions brought us to unfamiliar places and sights. Notable is the tequila plantation, which several families own and operate. The tasting experience was amazing; you would have thought that eight sips of the various tequila flavors would have made for a boisterous return trip – but no! Retire-Agers™ abounded on this cruise, so the bus drive and tour guide had a noticeably quiet ride – as we passengers were all asleep!

It was a good thing the next day was at sea, so we all had the chance to recuperate from the tequila experience!

Finally, we reached Panama City with a shore excursion to see the sights and explore the city. That night, everyone was excited as we awaited the next day's adventure: The Panama Canal.

Early morning risers, all of us. We did not want to waste a minute experiencing the canal transit. The front of the ship was crowded as lots of people were outside on the upper decks; some were in the food court which faced the front and had wide open windows. The Pacific Ocean entered the canal waterway. The first lock began as we watched the water being lowered ahead of us, the gates being opened as we sailed through. This happened several times as we passed each lock and sailed into the lake and rivers. Beautiful scenery along the way, very serene and tropical. Going under three bridges, at the end of a long day of the canal passage, we finally reached the Atlantic Ocean. Wow, what a journey!

What sights we had seen! What memories this experience brought to us! And, we have the Panama Canal Transit certificates as proof!

Cartegena, Columbia was our early morning stop the next day, and off we went on another shore excursion. This one was the best of the tours offering city sights, including old churches and other historical places, fortress climbing, a cultural show with amazing performances, going through a replica of the old emerald mines, and stopping at squares and centers among the local people. Watching the busy street scenes, old churches, and other historical places, etc. was the highlight of this trip.

Meeting the people on the ship was a trip in and of itself! Each night, we sat with different people and/or with friends we made along the way. After a few days, faces became familiar, and we hailed each other like old friends. We sat together during the nightly shows in the theater, we lounged together in the various sitting areas located throughout the ship, and we waved to each other at the casino as we played at different tables. So nice to spend time with them and to exchange contact information.

We disembarked in Ft. Lauderdale, Florida, and as we taxied to our hotel, Zaf sighed and said, "Well another thing to scratch off of our bucket list." Indeed. Relaxing by the pool at the hotel for a few days gave us the time to talk about where we wanted to go next. Remembering conversations we had with our fellow shipmates, we pondered: Australia? South Pacific? The Canadian Rockies? Back to Europe, Spain, and Portugal? What we will do next is in the works as we explore diverse options.

Exploring retirement is high on our agenda. We have finally reached a point in our lives where we can do a variety of things based on health, finances, and how we want to spend our time. Much gratitude is given each day because we can do so.

WHAT'S YOUR RETIREMENT SIZE?

Originally Published:

July 22, 2022

Your retirement size can be larger than life or small enough to keep you incredibly happy. I am not talking about your physical size, but your actual everyday living philosophy and actions. Some travel extensively all over the world; some join clubs or groups that have a considerable number of activities; others volunteer and do other philanthropic work. And yet, many choose to spend their time gardening, looking out their window while sipping a cup of tea at the glorious flowers they planted.

Let's face it. Over the years, our physical size has changed and most of us can say that, after a certain age, we gain weight and hope to lose it. The opposite is true in retirement. We gain perspective and wisdom… and hopefully, we do not lose it!

So many of us keep clothes that have become a bit tight because we are "planning" on losing the pounds that have accumulated. I have heard of women who had two sets of clothes in their wardrobe – one larger than the other so they would always have something to wear that fits properly.

Retirement can be like that. We dream of the day we can retire and do the things we want to do which work and other obligations prevented us from doing. Over the years, I have tucked away notes and information about cooking and gardening. I started my "memoir." I would close my eyes and envision grand trips to faraway places. This pre-planning was my extra-large size of things I wanted to do but did not fit into them yet.

And now that I am semi-retired, these things do not necessarily look good on me for a variety of reasons. Energy and desire have waned. Mornings are for getting my part-time work done and household chores and errands… that is when I am most bouncy and agile! The original idea was to get those tasks out of the way, so I could explore a new recipe, join a dance class, meet up with friends, or plant another lovely flower. But right after lunch, I have no zip left. I lie down to read and catnap.

Upon waking, I take one more spin around the house to see what else I can do that doesn't require much effort and then begin dinner, followed by a little TV watching. My husband Zaf is the boss of the remote control, so after we watch our game shows and a bit of news, he picks the movie or watches sports. I don't usually mind as I play my brain games on the iPad while he zaps his way through the channels. The voracious reader that I am, once in bed, I read and read. And often, when I wake up in the morning, I find my glasses askew on my forehead!

We certainly do travel, but the hassle of the actual traveling – airports and such – is a downer. We love it when we are at our destination, but prepping, packing, and transportation is often a deterrent. This is true no matter what size of travel we are interested in. And then again, the money issue. "Deals" are offered everywhere, but when you look at them closely, they are not always so great. So much is out there, and it gives me a headache going through them all to see how good a fit they are. And did you notice when you check out one little thing online, you are driven crazy by the number of ads from everyone in the universe about their own deal? What a nuisance!

Indeed, our finances are another way where the size we want to be is not a reality for many of us. What a huge awakening it is to realize that money is the undercurrent of what we can and cannot do. It curtails our activities when we see how far the dollar does not go. This affects most retirees, according to the latest statistics. So many posts on social media ask the question, "How much money do I need to retire?" Just like the people who want to start a business have asked me over the years: "How much money do I need to start my business?" The answer is the same. "It varies," I say. Where do you live? How much do you have? What do you want to do? It is not a one-size-fits-all solution.

And let us not forget other activities – walking, bowling, tennis, golf, volunteering, etc. – you can choose how often and to what degree. Small is enough to get you started – much like we were once upon a time. Medium is next – more activities or more time and money spent doing them. Growing into a larger size can sneak up on us … chairing a committee or golf tournament are two good examples of being totally immersed in more time-consuming pursuits. The happy part is we can try on each size and determine if it looks good on us. And the beauty of it is, just like buying a shirt and bringing it home only to decide that it really is not right for you, you can change sizes any time you want!

Time spent exploring what the next size might involve is time well spent. Do I have the energy to play golf more than once a week? Can I spend more time gardening and growing the entire backyard into a plethora of flora and fauna? Do Zaf and I really want to be on the road again and see the world? Each search should bring you enough information on what to expect… size does matter when we consider our mind, body, and soul. Having fun, enjoying your retirement life, and bringing yourself joy is what matters… not the size. You look gorgeous exactly as you are!

Whatever your retirement size is, small – medium – large – extra-large – wear it in good health!

ALOHA

Originally Published:

December 28, 2022

One of the topics of conversation among soon-to-be-retired people is the hope of traveling once they have the time to do so. After decades of work, raising a family, and maintaining a household, they are looking forward to taking off whenever they want to. It was certainly what Zaf and I were planning to do and indeed succeeded when we spent six months in Greece last year.

The retirement groups I follow on social media get numerous postings from people who are days, weeks, or months away from retirement and are expressing their desire to see the places that are on their "bucket list." Family and friends who are at this point in their lives also state they are getting ready to go, go, go. And rightly so, all these people should be planning to do just that as they earned it and deserve it.

The experience we had living in Greece last year was truly an anomaly. At the height of the pandemic, we vaccinated, we tested, we masked, and took off. The country was practically empty of tourists. Hotels, car rental, food, etc. were very inexpensive. This year, from what I heard from family and friends who visited there claimed that the current prices were exorbitant!

And that brings me to the issue of the cost of travel today, especially for us who have retired.

Exploring travel options for us is an eye-opener. With limited income, for most of us, there is only so much we can do. Now that the world has opened (no pandemic), prices have skyrocketed. We experienced that when we were in Hawaii last month. While it has always been on the more expensive side, this year was truly unbelievable.

We had breakfast in our room. A kitchenette was in our room with coffee included. We bought muffins and fruit, and that took care of that. A "light" lunch was about $40.00! When you looked at the menu, we saw that a hot dog was $20! At first, we thought, well that it was because we were sitting around the pool; when lunchtime rolled around, we were a captive audience. But then, when we ventured into town on another day and stopped for lunch, it was about the same!

Dinner was even worse. No matter what we ordered, the meal, along with beverages came in at about $100. Averaging about $150 a day for food, for six days, came to $900!!!

Adding in the cost of hotel and car rental, gas, and whatnot, this vacation for six days was equal to what we spent in Greece last year for one month! And this did not include airfare!

There are, of course, other destinations that might not be at that price level. Doing your research well ahead of time and knowing what to expect is necessary for good planning. Group travel is an option that could possibly be a better way to travel, cost-wise. Driving instead of flying might work as well; but with the price of gas, it might not be such a bargain. And, of course, you can't drive to Hawaii, Alaska, Europe, etc. The key for us is knowing what our budget is and what we can fit into it. You need money to travel the world… is our new mantra.

Hawaii is beautiful, no doubt about it. From the minute we landed, we were in another mental state – it automatically becomes more relaxed and stress-free. Not that we have so much angst, being retired and all, but you know… life has challenges no matter what. Endless beaches, palm trees, and other foliage in full bloom, the warmth of the sun, mountains in the background, and that certain ukulele music playing in the background puts you in a place where you don't want to leave.

Will we travel again soon? Yes, we will. Two places we will be visiting are driving destinations. Both hotel rooms will have kitchenettes. Packing includes snacks and beverages we can keep in our room to ward off hunger pains. Searching for moderately-priced restaurants in the area will keep costs down. So, we are ready. We are contemplating another trip to Europe next year… but who knows? We'll see what we can explore and discover. Blessed to be able to do so indeed!

RETIREMENT TODAY

Our Latest Travels as of

June 1, 2024

Well, we returned from our 6-month trip to Greece. We settled into our new home, have traveled a bit more, and we continue to live life large.

Our days vary… some are super busy and some are totally laid back. I continue to do a bit of work each morning – something I like and do not like at the same time. When I do not like it, I try to remember that it brings in the funds we need to continue to travel and explore. Our personal needs are met right after I finish work - paying bills, shopping for food and supplies, cleaning the house, doing laundry, and the like.

The good news is that I am typically done by noon, which leaves the rest of the day to do interesting things. Our development – where we live - affords us a variety of things to do. Zaf plays pickleball and golf, I go to the book club discussions, and together we play mahjong and attend weekly game nights where we meet up with our neighbors for an evening of cards or board games. This week, I am joining the group for a tour of a garden orchard followed by lunch. Monthly events bring the entire community together where we celebrate the 4th of July, Memorial Day, Super Bowl Sunday, and the like. Walking groups allow for some exercise right here in the development so we do not even need to walk on city streets. We pick and choose what we attend based on our own schedule, energy level, and interest.

Health and wellness means appointments with doctors and dentists. We are vigilant about this and get regular check-ups. Building up stamina to stay active is our goal - especially true for travel where we walk endlessly. Some airports are huge and getting from one gate to another is a challenge!

Visiting family is a big priority. Nothing brings joy to our lives more than seeing the faces we love and spending time with them. Some live nearby and some need some traveling, but we do it, nevertheless.

I am happy to report that we returned to Greece in 2023. After a Mediterranean cruise, we flew to Thessaloniki, rented a car, and took off to explore new parts of this beautiful country that we had never seen before. Terribly disappointed that we only had one month to do this when last time in 2021, we were there for six months! We also visited Hawaii and took a Panama Canal Cruise visiting Mexico, Costa Rica, Panama, and Columbia in 2022. Drives to Palm Desert, San Diego, Las Vegas, and Phoenix give us a "travel" feeling although these places are relatively close to where we live.

One of the things we have embraced is our church community. We have made great friends there and find a kindred spirit with each of them as we not only celebrate our faith together but our Greek heritage as well. The annual Greek festival keeps us hopping, as Zaf and I have taken on much responsibility for producing this event. During the event, we enjoy hearing the music, listening to people speaking our first language, relishing our ethnic food, and dancing to the sounds we remember so well. Our hearts are filled with pride and joy!

Retirement has taken its own road. When we were considering retirement, it did not look like the life we are living now. Somehow, at that time, in remembering parents and other older people, it seemed more sedentary. Long hours in front of the TV or sitting at the table over a cup of coffee with friends who were retired as well as talking about health, their children and grandchildren, and remembering the old days.

We, on the other hand, planned our journey to Greece where we bought our new house in a new city… but the rest of it was unknown. We knew we wanted to continue to travel, but it was more of an idea than a reality at the time. And now, after two and a half years into retirement, we see that retirement is of its own making. We are grateful that exploring retirement is key in our lives which brings us new experiences and much joy. We are grateful that our health still allows us to journey out into the world, although we are mindful of how we travel and where we travel.

Long-winded tours are not for us… nor is walking through ancient ruins that are enormous and complicated. We pick the places we want to visit, use lots of local transportation, and leave plenty of time to rest and relax. Adjustments yes, but we are not yet ready to throw in the towel to travel. What we have learned the most about retirement is that it is not to be feared. Being connected to some retirement groups, I often read that some people are apprehensive and anxious about letting go of their jobs and facing each day differently. I wish I could tell them, "GO AHEAD AND DO IT!" Of course, it depends on their finances and ability to care for themselves as they age. I realize that. And then again, I read that some people have done just that and it is the greatest thing that ever happened to them!

Those are the people who embraced this new chapter in their lives and made the most of it. A friend who lives nearby was planning to travel the world with her husband; alas, he passed on and she, rather than dwell in her sorrow, has joined a travel group and is out there, in the world, several times a year… to India, to Iceland, to Japan, etc. She has found what works for her and as she told me, this is how she remembers her husband and how much he would have loved visiting those places, too.

Do we fear the future? Yes and no. First, the no: we are blessed with the desire and ability to do what we want. And yes: we do not know how long we can continue to do so.

The one thing I know for sure is that Zaf and I have Retired Well.

THANK YOU FOR EXPLORING WITH US!

My wish for you is that you too Retire Well.

Mrs. Helene K. Liatsos-Tsimahides
2024
California, USA